CORRELATIONS®
Square Roots

EASY

WILLIAM S. ROGERS III

iUniverse, Inc.
Bloomington

Square Roots - Easy

iUniverse books may be ordered through booksellers or by contacting:

iUniverse
1663 Liberty Drive
Bloomington, IN 47403
www.iuniverse.com
1-800-Authors (1-800-288-4677)

ISBN: 978-1-4759-7910-7 (sc)
ISBN: 978-1-4759-7911-4 (ebk)

Printed in the United States of America

iUniverse rev. date: 02/22/2013

CORRELATIONS

Dear Consumer,

Congratulations! You have just purchased a one of a kind puzzle that is geared towards education while also having fun. I have worked diligently to create a style of puzzle that is different from the rest and that would stand out easily above all the others. Correlations is a puzzle that is educational and equipped to enhance the minds of others. This style of puzzle originated out of the thought of making math fun. I wanted to create a puzzle that would help people learn or re-learn the basic math concepts and create different levels in which people could try to conquer. Correlations is suitable for all ages of people whether young or old. This puzzle can be formatted for those who want to take it easy and for those who like a little challenge.

Correlations is like an enhanced mathematical word search. I have enjoyed bringing this new style of puzzle to the market, and I hope you enjoy doing this puzzle as much as I have enjoyed creating it. Nothing is too hard to do if you just set your mind to it. Correlations is going to challenge you when it comes to math and searching for the words within the puzzle. Congratulations once again, and I hope you have a blast on your Correlations journey!

William S. Rogers III

How to Solve Correlations

- The puzzles consist of a 7x7 grid
- Solve the math within the box and try to figure out what letters go where
- You do this by knowing where each letter falls in the alphabet (EX: A=1, K=11, P=16, T=20)
- EX: To find the letter G you would look for $\sqrt{49}$. The square root is 7=G
- Once you figure this out you have to find the words within the puzzle
- EX: GREEK – the words are not all straight or diagonal. As long as the G is touching the R box, the R is touching the E box, the E is touching the E box, and the E is touching the K box then the word is found within the puzzle
- The letters within the puzzles are only used once (**NO ONE LETTER OR BOX CAN BE USED TWICE**)
- All the boxes within the puzzle are not to be filled
- (1) (2) (3) (4) · These are used to identify the words on the Answer Sheets

Take this 7 X 7-square example on this page

√225	√256=P (4)	√9	√16	√196	√400	√169
√9	√324=R (4)	√225=O (4)	√49	√64	√121	√441
√25=E (4)	√361=S (4)	√441	√1	√9	√25	√144
√400=T (4)	√400=T (1)	√36	√25=E (1)	√529=W (2)	√400=T (3)	√49
√441	√144=L (1)	√196=N (1)	√225=O (2)	√49=G (1)	√144	√441=U (3)
√1	√9	√25=E (1)	√16=D (2)	√9=C (3)	√25=E (2)	√196=N (3)
√16	√324	√9=C (3)	√225=O (3)	√1=A (2)	√225=O (3)	√169=M (2)

WORDS

1. GENTLE (7, 5, 14, 20, 12, 5)
2. MEADOW (13, 5, 1, 4, 15, 23)
3. COCONUT (3, 15, 3, 15, 14, 21, 20)
4. POSTER (16, 15, 19, 20, 5, 18)

To start, look for a word that have letters that are not in the other words. The word MEADOW; locate the letter M first by looking for √169. The square root comes out to be 13, which M is the 13th letter in the alphabet. There are 2 √169 boxes, one in the upper right hand corner and one in the lower right hand corner. Next, try to locate √25 which would be E. This is the next letter in the word MEADOW. There is only one box that has √25 that is connected to the box that contains √169. The box in the lower right hand corner is the box that works. After, look for the A which would be √1. The box that contains √16=D would be next in line to follow after the A is found. Now, from here you can either go up or down because both of the boxes contain √225=O. When a situation like this arises, you have to plan ahead and look for the next letter which would be √529=W. The box at the bottom does not have √529 connected to it. So therefore, it has to be the √225 box up above. From here, the √529=W is diagonal from this box. The word MEADOW is now found within the puzzle.

Once a word is found in the puzzle, those boxes can't be used once again. This is called the Elimination Process. Before you try and make a move to figure out where the next letter is within a word, look around in each direction and look for possible solutions. Often times there may be more than one box with the letter that you are looking for. When this occurs, try and plan out where each letter is and make sure that the letters are not in other words. The numbers below the square roots in the box correlates to what word that letter goes to.

If one discovers that a word is too hard to find, locate part of the word within the puzzle first, stop, and search for a new word. This often helps because searching for a new word can eliminate some of the boxes that you may have thought were going to be used for the first word you were searching for. There is no guess work that needs to be done when it comes to these puzzles. All you have to do is solve the math, plan ahead, look at the surrounding boxes, and figure out where the words are within the puzzle. Use these tips in order to continue finding the rest of the words within the puzzle.

Additional Tips

- Try to solve the math within the box to find the words within the puzzle
- Try and look for letters that are not in other words
- In puzzles that have similar letters within words, try and find the letters that are the same (It sometimes help to look for a word backwards, starting with the last letter in the word)
- Remember, you can only use a box once; so try and plan ahead

Square Roots

A=1 $\sqrt{1}$
B=2 $\sqrt{4}$
C=3 $\sqrt{9}$
D=4 $\sqrt{16}$
E=5 $\sqrt{25}$
F=6 $\sqrt{36}$
G=7 $\sqrt{49}$
H=8 $\sqrt{64}$
I=9 $\sqrt{81}$
J=10 $\sqrt{100}$
K=11 $\sqrt{121}$
L=12 $\sqrt{144}$
M=13 $\sqrt{169}$

N=14 $\sqrt{196}$
O=15 $\sqrt{225}$
P=16 $\sqrt{256}$
Q=17 $\sqrt{289}$
R=18 $\sqrt{324}$
S=19 $\sqrt{361}$
T=20 $\sqrt{400}$
U=21 $\sqrt{441}$
V=22 $\sqrt{484}$
W=23 $\sqrt{529}$
X=24 $\sqrt{576}$
Y=25 $\sqrt{625}$
Z=26 $\sqrt{676}$

EASY

√1	√625	√121	√225	√324	√121	√100
√361	√36	√4	√81	√25	√324	√49
√16	√4	√25	√400	√144	√81	√36
√9	√196	√1	√400	√16	√256	√49
√144	√4	√25	√144	√16	√81	√324
√441	√81	√400	√361	√144	√324	√529
√25	√361	√256	√25	√225	√676	√400

WORDS

1. BABIES
2. RIDDLE
3. KITTEN
4. TRIPLE

EASY

√121	√9	√361	√225	√441	√676	√576
√81	√36	√324	√49	√16	√256	√144
√4	√25	√81	√361	√196	√1	√121
√25	√64	√441	√4	√324	√81	√361
√64	√400	√1	√64	√1	√49	√324
√225	√256	√196	√25	√9	√256	√1
√144	√16	√144	√441	√25	√529	√576

WORDS

1. HANDLE
2. PARACHUTE
3. AGING
4. CRIBS

EASY

√144	√441	√225	√256	√49	√64	√100
√529	√625	√676	√9	√16	√361	√9
√225	√441	√81	√121	√144	√1	√25
√256	√36	√25	√196	√25	√196	√144
√16	√144	√225	√289	√49	√4	√9
√9	√25	√529	√100	√196	√1	√25
√49	√144	√529	√81	√9	√324	√81

WORDS

1. KNOWING
2. YIELD
3. CANCER
4. CABLES

EASY

√121	√64	√49	√81	√144	√256	√49
√225	√625	√676	√25	√9	√196	√49
√324	√361	√36	√25	√256	√81	√196
√361	√25	√324	√169	√144	√81	√100
√4	√1	√169	√1	√25	√36	√121
√169	√81	√81	√196	√9	√100	√25
√144	√361	√144	√400	√324	√256	√225

WORDS

1. FEELING
2. LIARS
3. CAMPING
4. TIMERS

EASY

√625	√25	√49	√81	√121	√441	√484
√81	√625	√64	√256	√361	√225	√324
√64	√144	√1	√1	√169	√361	√625
√361	√576	√324	√676	√81	√256	√25
√36	√324	√16	√196	√256	√25	√400
√441	√64	√225	√225	√1	√144	√1
√4	√25	√36	√441	√4	√64	√121

WORDS

1. DOUBLE
2. MINORS
3. HARASS
4. HAPPY

EASY

$\sqrt{81}$	$\sqrt{144}$	$\sqrt{25}$	$\sqrt{49}$	$\sqrt{100}$	$\sqrt{441}$	$\sqrt{625}$
$\sqrt{676}$	$\sqrt{81}$	$\sqrt{1}$	$\sqrt{4}$	$\sqrt{361}$	$\sqrt{25}$	$\sqrt{1}$
$\sqrt{36}$	$\sqrt{121}$	$\sqrt{324}$	$\sqrt{81}$	$\sqrt{324}$	$\sqrt{484}$	$\sqrt{144}$
$\sqrt{361}$	$\sqrt{196}$	$\sqrt{16}$	$\sqrt{196}$	$\sqrt{4}$	$\sqrt{25}$	$\sqrt{144}$
$\sqrt{25}$	$\sqrt{144}$	$\sqrt{256}$	$\sqrt{49}$	$\sqrt{196}$	$\sqrt{25}$	$\sqrt{400}$
$\sqrt{36}$	$\sqrt{169}$	$\sqrt{1}$	$\sqrt{144}$	$\sqrt{225}$	$\sqrt{400}$	$\sqrt{196}$
$\sqrt{400}$	$\sqrt{441}$	$\sqrt{324}$	$\sqrt{361}$	$\sqrt{25}$	$\sqrt{361}$	$\sqrt{225}$

WORDS

1. LARSON
2. SINGLE
3. LEARNS
4. LETTER

EASY

$\sqrt{64}$	$\sqrt{225}$	$\sqrt{16}$	$\sqrt{169}$	$\sqrt{400}$	$\sqrt{81}$	$\sqrt{9}$
$\sqrt{4}$	$\sqrt{16}$	$\sqrt{25}$	$\sqrt{36}$	$\sqrt{25}$	$\sqrt{256}$	$\sqrt{36}$
$\sqrt{49}$	$\sqrt{144}$	$\sqrt{225}$	$\sqrt{196}$	$\sqrt{400}$	$\sqrt{81}$	$\sqrt{324}$
$\sqrt{400}$	$\sqrt{25}$	$\sqrt{81}$	$\sqrt{441}$	$\sqrt{196}$	$\sqrt{25}$	$\sqrt{196}$
$\sqrt{25}$	$\sqrt{16}$	$\sqrt{49}$	$\sqrt{81}$	$\sqrt{256}$	$\sqrt{25}$	$\sqrt{49}$
$\sqrt{81}$	$\sqrt{676}$	$\sqrt{25}$	$\sqrt{361}$	$\sqrt{361}$	$\sqrt{529}$	$\sqrt{81}$
$\sqrt{49}$	$\sqrt{529}$	$\sqrt{625}$	$\sqrt{1}$	$\sqrt{676}$	$\sqrt{81}$	$\sqrt{9}$

WORDS

1. ESSAY
2. OUTING
3. DINNER
4. DELETE

EASY

$\sqrt{289}$	$\sqrt{4}$	$\sqrt{400}$	$\sqrt{25}$	$\sqrt{36}$	$\sqrt{121}$	$\sqrt{100}$
$\sqrt{400}$	$\sqrt{1}$	$\sqrt{25}$	$\sqrt{324}$	$\sqrt{324}$	$\sqrt{441}$	$\sqrt{64}$
$\sqrt{36}$	$\sqrt{144}$	$\sqrt{529}$	$\sqrt{400}$	$\sqrt{25}$	$\sqrt{361}$	$\sqrt{9}$
$\sqrt{625}$	$\sqrt{169}$	$\sqrt{25}$	$\sqrt{1}$	$\sqrt{169}$	$\sqrt{361}$	$\sqrt{81}$
$\sqrt{400}$	$\sqrt{361}$	$\sqrt{441}$	$\sqrt{144}$	$\sqrt{81}$	$\sqrt{400}$	$\sqrt{361}$
$\sqrt{169}$	$\sqrt{196}$	$\sqrt{49}$	$\sqrt{196}$	$\sqrt{25}$	$\sqrt{484}$	$\sqrt{9}$
$\sqrt{121}$	$\sqrt{144}$	$\sqrt{36}$	$\sqrt{49}$	$\sqrt{324}$	$\sqrt{289}$	$\sqrt{81}$

WORDS

1. MERELY
2. RELATE
3. STINGS
4. WATERS

EASY

√361	√25	√36	√16	√121	√361	√49
√64	√4	√196	√225	√361	√400	√81
√441	√625	√1	√144	√676	√324	√36
√1	√64	√9	√324	√16	√81	√625
√576	√9	√81	√441	√49	√25	√64
√361	√324	√196	√49	√225	√144	√324
√361	√225	√25	√49	√256	√324	√361

WORDS

1. POURING
2. TRIGGERS
3. FOLDER
4. HANDS

EASY

√361	√121	√81	√169	√144	√625	√529
√225	√256	√9	√625	√676	√81	√9
√100	√361	√324	√196	√324	√361	√49
√64	√225	√225	√196	√361	√256	√9
√225	√361	√81	√196	√25	√121	√225
√144	√225	√400	√9	√256	√144	√36
√9	√100	√256	√400	√25	√144	√441

WORDS

1. MICROS
2. PENNY
3. COINS
4. COLLECT

EASY

√1	√441	√324	√49	√361	√81	√121
√144	√169	√361	√196	√225	√16	√256
√441	√400	√1	√529	√676	√25	√324
√361	√576	√225	√36	√9	√1	√361
√25	√1	√441	√25	√64	√400	√225
√9	√25	√196	√400	√361	√225	√361
√81	√16	√169	√441	√625	√529	√441

WORDS

1. CHOOSE
2. SAFETY
3. MUSTARD
4. SAND

EASY

√441	√121	√484	√529	√196	√676	√25
√196	√144	√25	√81	√49	√361	√1
√9	√16	√225	√121	√256	√1	√49
√225	√25	√81	√256	√36	√196	√196
√36	√4	√324	√225	√16	√81	√49
√81	√1	√225	√4	√144	√9	√529
√100	√121	√324	√361	√676	√25	√625

WORDS

1. SANDLE
2. UNDER
3. ROOFING
4. BIKING

EASY

√144	√256	√49	√225	√441	√484	√100
√25	√196	√16	√144	√36	√49	√324
√361	√144	√81	√625	√49	√25	√121
√324	√16	√4	√256	√16	√256	√256
√289	√225	√81	√225	√144	√9	√81
√169	√196	√529	√1	√64	√1	√169
√400	√25	√9	√400	√256	√64	√49

WORDS

1. WORLDLY
2. CAPTAIN
3. HOPING
4. PIPER

EASY

√144	√256	√49	√81	√441	√361	√625
√529	√25	√36	√1	√400	√25	√225
√441	√49	√400	√49	√1	√324	√16
√4	√324	√196	√49	√25	√144	√25
√576	√441	√81	√81	√64	√400	√16
√121	√169	√256	√16	√324	√225	√144
√361	√25	√64	√225	√144	√576	√529

WORDS

1. HOLDING
2. BRIGHT
3. OLDER
4. ELDEST

EASY

√576	√625	√36	√25	√4	√361	√121
√324	√1	√49	√169	√49	√144	√25
√625	√64	√441	√196	√196	√625	√256
√81	√324	√81	√81	√1	√81	√9
√9	√169	√49	√484	√529	√225	√16
√4	√1	√81	√64	√49	√9	√81
√676	√4	√144	√121	√289	√225	√256

WORDS

1. HIGHWAY
2. LIVING
3. DOING
4. CRUMBLE

EASY

√225	√36	√25	√1	√16	√361	√484
√441	√4	√256	√529	√625	√25	√400
√361	√144	√225	√49	√64	√324	√361
√9	√25	√81	√324	√9	√324	√36
√676	√324	√81	√196	√25	√324	√576
√25	√4	√256	√64	√441	√81	√9
√121	√400	√9	√400	√441	√64	√49

WORDS

1. SCRIPT
2. LINERS
3. CHURCH
4. POWDER

EASY

$\sqrt{36}$	$\sqrt{256}$	$\sqrt{36}$	$\sqrt{121}$	$\sqrt{361}$	$\sqrt{400}$	$\sqrt{441}$
$\sqrt{9}$	$\sqrt{225}$	$\sqrt{225}$	$\sqrt{256}$	$\sqrt{196}$	$\sqrt{324}$	$\sqrt{484}$
$\sqrt{529}$	$\sqrt{196}$	$\sqrt{400}$	$\sqrt{361}$	$\sqrt{81}$	$\sqrt{676}$	$\sqrt{81}$
$\sqrt{9}$	$\sqrt{361}$	$\sqrt{441}$	$\sqrt{196}$	$\sqrt{64}$	$\sqrt{1}$	$\sqrt{121}$
$\sqrt{100}$	$\sqrt{441}$	$\sqrt{324}$	$\sqrt{256}$	$\sqrt{400}$	$\sqrt{256}$	$\sqrt{4}$
$\sqrt{25}$	$\sqrt{361}$	$\sqrt{4}$	$\sqrt{361}$	$\sqrt{49}$	$\sqrt{441}$	$\sqrt{324}$
$\sqrt{9}$	$\sqrt{121}$	$\sqrt{324}$	$\sqrt{25}$	$\sqrt{144}$	$\sqrt{64}$	$\sqrt{676}$

WORDS

1. FONTS
2. PAINT
3. BRUSH
4. RULERS

EASY

√25	√441	√1	√484	√81	√169	√196
√324	√225	√256	√196	√49	√4	√441
√324	√81	√1	√25	√25	√361	√196
√100	√1	√196	√144	√324	√121	√441
√576	√1	√256	√361	√256	√676	√81
√9	√4	√25	√441	√169	√484	√400
√25	√81	√9	√121	√196	√1	√529

WORDS

1. NUMBERS
2. PAIR
3. AMPLE
4. BANANA

EASY

$\sqrt{121}$	$\sqrt{361}$	$\sqrt{49}$	$\sqrt{81}$	$\sqrt{100}$	$\sqrt{25}$	$\sqrt{4}$
$\sqrt{9}$	$\sqrt{484}$	$\sqrt{676}$	$\sqrt{625}$	$\sqrt{361}$	$\sqrt{144}$	$\sqrt{361}$
$\sqrt{529}$	$\sqrt{4}$	$\sqrt{169}$	$\sqrt{256}$	$\sqrt{324}$	$\sqrt{361}$	$\sqrt{4}$
$\sqrt{1}$	$\sqrt{9}$	$\sqrt{1}$	$\sqrt{25}$	$\sqrt{81}$	$\sqrt{64}$	$\sqrt{225}$
$\sqrt{49}$	$\sqrt{144}$	$\sqrt{64}$	$\sqrt{9}$	$\sqrt{225}$	$\sqrt{100}$	$\sqrt{64}$
$\sqrt{196}$	$\sqrt{9}$	$\sqrt{225}$	$\sqrt{1}$	$\sqrt{144}$	$\sqrt{196}$	$\sqrt{169}$
$\sqrt{25}$	$\sqrt{81}$	$\sqrt{484}$	$\sqrt{256}$	$\sqrt{36}$	$\sqrt{441}$	$\sqrt{576}$

WORDS

1. CHAMPION
2. PACERS
3. LOVING
4. JOBLESS

EASY

√441	√25	√676	√25	√169	√576	√529
√225	√400	√4	√1	√256	√49	√9
√4	√324	√324	√25	√196	√9	√1
√25	√441	√81	√1	√324	√49	√64
√676	√484	√9	√400	√9	√16	√25
√4	√16	√25	√144	√64	√121	√196
√225	√256	√81	√49	√81	√100	√625

WORDS

1. CREAM
2. DELIGHT
3. BRANCH
4. VIRTUE

EASY

√441	√400	√484	√49	√9	√81	√121
√144	√324	√225	√256	√196	√361	√676
√324	√441	√100	√484	√81	√625	√576
√361	√25	√169	√169	√1	√400	√49
√484	√576	√441	√4	√36	√144	√16
√25	√64	√225	√324	√81	√441	√25
√49	√81	√121	√49	√16	√361	√144

WORDS

1. VALUE
2. HUMMING
3. GRIDS
4. BOXES

EASY

√361	√49	√121	√9	√100	√81	√324
√361	√441	√1	√64	√49	√64	√121
√25	√400	√81	√144	√196	√36	√49
√225	√196	√144	√256	√81	√49	√196
√25	√36	√225	√16	√400	√81	√64
√49	√169	√1	√361	√400	√100	√1
√9	√441	√25	√361	√1	√144	√4

WORDS

1. FASTING
2. CHILD
3. LASTING
4. MENTAL

EASY

√121	√441	√529	√576	√676	√64	√81
√9	√121	√144	√225	√169	√256	√64
√225	√676	√81	√9	√400	√25	√49
√49	√36	√121	√324	√64	√144	√81
√196	√81	√361	√361	√25	√16	√25
√196	√81	√144	√81	√361	√1	√196
√16	√400	√196	√49	√9	√1	√256

WORDS

1. PASSING
2. FINDING
3. OTHERS
4. CANDLE

EASY

√256	√121	√16	√100	√4	√81	√256
√225	√4	√25	√4	√441	√144	√25
√484	√576	√225	√81	√625	√9	√529
√676	√49	√4	√324	√144	√1	√25
√144	√169	√64	√81	√324	√196	√81
√25	√361	√1	√400	√1	√9	√16
√121	√196	√4	√256	√16	√144	√324

WORDS

1. THANKS
2. CARRIED
3. DAILY
4. BOBBLE

EASY

√64	√144	√484	√400	√9	√25	√25
√100	√25	√121	√144	√324	√169	√16
√25	√144	√9	√1	√324	√529	√576
√256	√9	√64	√225	√361	√676	√625
√81	√1	√361	√36	√64	√1	√64
√4	√9	√25	√81	√196	√4	√25
√144	√196	√400	√16	√81	√169	√81

WORDS

1. CLASH
2. TEACH
3. INFORMED
4. DISCIPLE

EASY

√144	√324	√361	√225	√144	√256	√36
√25	√49	√324	√81	√25	√1	√9
√81	√25	√196	√400	√121	√25	√49
√144	√121	√16	√441	√324	√100	√324
√361	√169	√256	√196	√1	√9	√49
√64	√225	√529	√169	√81	√4	√576
√9	√625	√225	√256	√676	√81	√121

WORDS

1. MARKING
2. BINDER
3. COMPUTE
4. REAL

EASY

√144	√25	√196	√49	√324	√1	√16
√49	√121	√81	√361	√144	√25	√324
√361	√81	√441	√49	√64	√400	√361
√64	√256	√225	√49	√64	√25	√676
√625	√529	√441	√1	√49	√625	√4
√25	√4	√4	√400	√81	√144	√196
√196	√225	√400	√289	√625	√225	√289

WORDS

1. BAGGING
2. LIGHTER
3. BUTTON
4. PUSHES

EASY

√81	√9	√121	√100	√324	√400	√441
√529	√676	√4	√25	√361	√36	√225
√256	√361	√400	√324	√289	√324	√121
√169	√324	√324	√1	√144	√25	√36
√16	√1	√25	√625	√144	√256	√529
√121	√400	√225	√144	√400	√441	√225
√441	√225	√361	√484	√25	√256	√225

WORDS

1. PLAYERS
2. STARTER
3. POWERS
4. OUTLOOK

EASY

√529	√121	√49	√196	√64	√576	√625
√676	√4	√4	√121	√81	√324	√9
√1	√121	√144	√256	√169	√25	√16
√196	√400	√25	√9	√484	√49	√441
√484	√361	√100	√361	√64	√324	√25
√361	√64	√25	√400	√225	√81	√144
√36	√1	√144	√9	√361	√144	√169

WORDS

1. CHRIST
2. BLESS
3. DRINK
4. COLLEGE

EASY

√324	√361	√400	√256	√81	√9	√16
√676	√441	√361	√225	√484	√25	√25
√4	√169	√400	√441	√324	√1	√361
√196	√81	√256	√324	√1	√324	√225
√324	√361	√169	√49	√25	√324	√36
√81	√1	√49	√196	√81	√64	√289
√9	√400	√49	√484	√25	√676	√625

WORDS

1. CAMPUS
2. HEART
3. EARRING
4. STORES

EASY

√441	√25	√64	√676	√196	√81	√529
√529	√4	√81	√169	√49	√144	√25
√196	√441	√225	√400	√324	√400	√324
√361	√324	√441	√25	√25	√196	√576
√529	√49	√676	√144	√441	√400	√36
√1	√64	√4	√1	√225	√361	√9
√400	√16	√256	√400	√225	√9	√324

WORDS

1. BOUGHT
2. STERLING
3. TABLE
4. COUNTER

EASY

$\sqrt{144}$	$\sqrt{400}$	$\sqrt{81}$	$\sqrt{25}$	$\sqrt{324}$	$\sqrt{441}$	$\sqrt{625}$
$\sqrt{529}$	$\sqrt{100}$	$\sqrt{676}$	$\sqrt{4}$	$\sqrt{225}$	$\sqrt{16}$	$\sqrt{25}$
$\sqrt{36}$	$\sqrt{225}$	$\sqrt{324}$	$\sqrt{361}$	$\sqrt{25}$	$\sqrt{9}$	$\sqrt{49}$
$\sqrt{1}$	$\sqrt{256}$	$\sqrt{441}$	$\sqrt{196}$	$\sqrt{9}$	$\sqrt{121}$	$\sqrt{64}$
$\sqrt{25}$	$\sqrt{16}$	$\sqrt{49}$	$\sqrt{16}$	$\sqrt{81}$	$\sqrt{81}$	$\sqrt{169}$
$\sqrt{196}$	$\sqrt{25}$	$\sqrt{81}$	$\sqrt{16}$	$\sqrt{81}$	$\sqrt{529}$	$\sqrt{196}$
$\sqrt{144}$	$\sqrt{441}$	$\sqrt{144}$	$\sqrt{361}$	$\sqrt{196}$	$\sqrt{484}$	$\sqrt{400}$

WORDS

1. ROCKING
2. TWICE
3. PUDDLE
4. INSIDE

EASY

√400	√225	√361	√25	√256	√64	√81
√49	√121	√49	√361	√361	√25	√9
√196	√484	√1	√576	√25	√49	√529
√81	√400	√625	√49	√324	√196	√25
√676	√324	√1	√121	√81	√16	√324
√576	√64	√1	√4	√225	√9	√256
√400	√441	√1	√9	√169	√361	√196

WORDS

1. DRESSES
2. TAKING
3. CARING
4. SCREW

EASY

√289	√16	√25	√225	√324	√361	√121
√144	√100	√144	√25	√196	√400	√441
√529	√625	√529	√49	√400	√361	√144
√25	√9	√400	√49	√441	√625	√1
√4	√25	√121	√225	√324	√324	√289
√25	√144	√256	√25	√49	√169	√400
√361	√169	√289	√4	√225	√256	√484

WORDS

1. TWENTY
2. GOGGLE
3. SEEKER
4. TRUST

EASY

√361	√225	√576	√625	√81	√100	√256
√25	√256	√484	√49	√225	√36	√25
√1	√324	√9	√144	√324	√529	√361
√16	√4	√1	√144	√676	√25	√400
√576	√144	√441	√225	√16	√225	√144
√169	√289	√25	√1	√36	√225	√196
√25	√144	√361	√289	√361	√256	√324

WORDS

1. FOLLOW
2. LEADER
3. SQUARE
4. ROOTS

EASY

$\sqrt{25}$	$\sqrt{9}$	$\sqrt{121}$	$\sqrt{100}$	$\sqrt{81}$	$\sqrt{196}$	$\sqrt{289}$
$\sqrt{256}$	$\sqrt{16}$	$\sqrt{4}$	$\sqrt{144}$	$\sqrt{4}$	$\sqrt{81}$	$\sqrt{49}$
$\sqrt{25}$	$\sqrt{256}$	$\sqrt{289}$	$\sqrt{144}$	$\sqrt{625}$	$\sqrt{25}$	$\sqrt{676}$
$\sqrt{625}$	$\sqrt{25}$	$\sqrt{324}$	$\sqrt{25}$	$\sqrt{1}$	$\sqrt{529}$	$\sqrt{25}$
$\sqrt{529}$	$\sqrt{144}$	$\sqrt{1}$	$\sqrt{196}$	$\sqrt{400}$	$\sqrt{81}$	$\sqrt{361}$
$\sqrt{324}$	$\sqrt{9}$	$\sqrt{400}$	$\sqrt{225}$	$\sqrt{196}$	$\sqrt{169}$	$\sqrt{400}$
$\sqrt{25}$	$\sqrt{441}$	$\sqrt{484}$	$\sqrt{49}$	$\sqrt{81}$	$\sqrt{64}$	$\sqrt{625}$

WORDS

1. WINNER
2. TOTALLY
3. PEACE
4. SEEING

EASY

√169	√144	√529	√144	√49	√64	√121
√100	√81	√484	√196	√25	√4	√16
√25	√36	√25	√81	√324	√64	√361
√144	√81	√361	√1	√361	√441	√64
√400	√676	√9	√25	√49	√225	√625
√529	√196	√81	√256	√144	√121	√441
√49	√9	√16	√225	√9	√256	√64

WORDS

1. CLEAR
2. ICING
3. HOUSING
4. SHELVES

EASY

√25	√49	√81	√121	√169	√256	√36
√4	√361	√36	√16	√25	√64	√64
√144	√121	√64	√49	√1	√1	√400
√361	√9	√25	√25	√324	√169	√169
√196	√16	√1	√324	√4	√1	√121
√529	√361	√625	√324	√225	√676	√16
√676	√64	√16	√9	√4	√256	√324

WORDS

1. HARBOR
2. SHEDS
3. DAMAGE
4. CRACKS

EASY

√289	√49	√324	√400	√36	√81	√144
√361	√144	√324	√25	√256	√36	√324
√484	√441	√25	√256	√1	√441	√676
√625	√225	√169	√361	√9	√529	√100
√625	√16	√1	√4	√196	√9	√16
√25	√225	√64	√144	√81	√225	√9
√289	√100	√256	√441	√484	√529	√676

WORDS

1. DAMPER
2. INSERT
3. JOYOUS
4. OCCUR

EASY

√169	√400	√529	√676	√81	√49	√144
√121	√529	√49	√64	√225	√36	√16
√9	√361	√196	√81	√36	√81	√25
√256	√4	√81	√4	√36	√36	√100
√1	√625	√9	√144	√400	√121	√81
√289	√144	√441	√4	√361	√625	√9
√324	√361	√49	√64	√100	√25	√361

WORDS

1. FIFTY
2. CLAPS
3. BUYING
4. OFFICE

EASY

√121	√4	√144	√25	√529	√625	√676
√324	√64	√361	√196	√144	√81	√49
√441	√81	√121	√81	√49	√225	√100
√9	√625	√144	√196	√16	√64	√25
√256	√25	√81	√400	√25	√4	√225
√324	√361	√144	√1	√289	√9	√400
√441	√484	√121	√169	√1	√144	√1

WORDS

1. MAILING
2. BENTLEY
3. ALCOHOL
4. BRUISE

EASY

√9	√100	√196	√25	√4	√225	√256
√625	√529	√49	√81	√9	√25	√36
√121	√36	√144	√16	√324	√289	√361
√49	√361	√81	√441	√1	√25	√64
√196	√225	√144	√81	√256	√49	√64
√9	√81	√144	√25	√361	√25	√4
√100	√361	√16	√400	√4	√1	√144

WORDS

1. CRUISE
2. FILING
3. HEADING
4. LABELS

EASY

√361	√144	√25	√36	√225	√49	√256
√529	√25	√625	√676	√81	√225	√9
√361	√64	√324	√1	√25	√4	√81
√361	√196	√361	√256	√169	√16	√196
√441	√196	√1	√144	√100	√49	√1
√256	√64	√25	√324	√400	√289	√324
√361	√324	√100	√1	√49	√64	√49

WORDS

1. USHERS
2. TRANS
3. HELPED
4. GOING

EASY

$\sqrt{25}$	$\sqrt{676}$	$\sqrt{49}$	$\sqrt{9}$	$\sqrt{81}$	$\sqrt{121}$	$\sqrt{169}$
$\sqrt{289}$	$\sqrt{4}$	$\sqrt{256}$	$\sqrt{1}$	$\sqrt{64}$	$\sqrt{81}$	$\sqrt{9}$
$\sqrt{4}$	$\sqrt{25}$	$\sqrt{225}$	$\sqrt{324}$	$\sqrt{1}$	$\sqrt{289}$	$\sqrt{49}$
$\sqrt{64}$	$\sqrt{36}$	$\sqrt{324}$	$\sqrt{81}$	$\sqrt{16}$	$\sqrt{25}$	$\sqrt{361}$
$\sqrt{289}$	$\sqrt{400}$	$\sqrt{324}$	$\sqrt{441}$	$\sqrt{121}$	$\sqrt{25}$	$\sqrt{100}$
$\sqrt{64}$	$\sqrt{676}$	$\sqrt{361}$	$\sqrt{361}$	$\sqrt{225}$	$\sqrt{576}$	$\sqrt{625}$
$\sqrt{529}$	$\sqrt{576}$	$\sqrt{49}$	$\sqrt{81}$	$\sqrt{36}$	$\sqrt{100}$	$\sqrt{81}$

WORDS

1. FOURTH
2. GEEKS
3. CHAIRS
4. BOARD

EASY

√441	√400	√196	√49	√324	√36	√49
√81	√100	√16	√81	√676	√576	√361
√144	√25	√256	√9	√196	√81	√9
√324	√676	√25	√81	√36	√196	√25
√49	√25	√256	√1	√324	√9	√81
√121	√324	√64	√400	√81	√256	√25
√441	√1	√9	√400	√121	√169	√196

WORDS

1. FATHERED
2. PRICE
3. SINNING
4. PRACTICE

EASY

$\sqrt{25}$	$\sqrt{441}$	$\sqrt{36}$	$\sqrt{25}$	$\sqrt{400}$	$\sqrt{576}$	$\sqrt{441}$
$\sqrt{400}$	$\sqrt{144}$	$\sqrt{625}$	$\sqrt{625}$	$\sqrt{25}$	$\sqrt{121}$	$\sqrt{1}$
$\sqrt{4}$	$\sqrt{256}$	$\sqrt{1}$	$\sqrt{361}$	$\sqrt{324}$	$\sqrt{64}$	$\sqrt{9}$
$\sqrt{25}$	$\sqrt{64}$	$\sqrt{400}$	$\sqrt{400}$	$\sqrt{225}$	$\sqrt{49}$	$\sqrt{441}$
$\sqrt{289}$	$\sqrt{324}$	$\sqrt{144}$	$\sqrt{361}$	$\sqrt{81}$	$\sqrt{144}$	$\sqrt{4}$
$\sqrt{361}$	$\sqrt{9}$	$\sqrt{49}$	$\sqrt{144}$	$\sqrt{64}$	$\sqrt{49}$	$\sqrt{49}$
$\sqrt{81}$	$\sqrt{49}$	$\sqrt{25}$	$\sqrt{81}$	$\sqrt{81}$	$\sqrt{196}$	$\sqrt{16}$

WORDS

1. STAPLE
2. GLORY
3. HIGHEST
4. CEILING

EASY

√196	√25	√441	√625	√529	√81	√361
√9	√16	√25	√225	√144	√16	√100
√256	√100	√144	√256	√225	√25	√1
√4	√225	√441	√25	√64	√324	√25
√9	√196	√16	√9	√324	√324	√361
√256	√225	√289	√361	√100	√4	√144
√169	√529	√81	√64	√4	√9	√225

WORDS

1. SCHOOL
2. COUPLE
3. WONDER
4. BREADS

EASY

√81	√100	√484	√9	√81	√676	√576
√64	√144	√25	√81	√49	√625	√36
√361	√400	√225	√324	√441	√400	√361
√4	√1	√25	√225	√81	√256	√49
√256	√289	√1	√324	√144	√196	√625
√576	√64	√49	√16	√81	√81	√1
√529	√81	√121	√100	√4	√16	√4

WORDS

1. ABILITY
2. READING
3. GROUPS
4. VIOLETS

EASY

√400	√484	√25	√256	√81	√49	√100
√144	√25	√361	√676	√576	√49	√529
√81	√625	√81	√169	√196	√1	√289
√25	√324	√144	√9	√25	√144	√361
√361	√400	√441	√484	√324	√324	√1
√9	√144	√25	√196	√25	√144	√576
√441	√484	√529	√169	√1	√625	√256

WORDS

1. SILVER
2. MERCURY
3. GALAXY
4. PLANETS

EASY

√121	√25	√256	√100	√196	√121	√400
√676	√9	√16	√361	√49	√81	√64
√121	√225	√49	√1	√196	√361	√676
√576	√196	√484	√196	√361	√9	√529
√81	√16	√121	√1	√225	√25	√169
√196	√64	√1	√36	√49	√324	√100
√441	√484	√576	√64	√529	√625	√9

WORDS

1. KNOCK
2. GANGS
3. ADVANCE
4. CROSSING

EASY

√121	√256	√529	√225	√36	√1	√400
√4	√81	√324	√100	√400	√64	√484
√625	√225	√676	√529	√625	√4	√49
√64	√196	√121	√144	√1	√144	√81
√49	√16	√25	√9	√1	√25	√324
√9	√324	√289	√64	√529	√324	√361
√64	√25	√121	√144	√324	√484	√441

WORDS

1. WALKER
2. BLEACH
3. WRONG
4. RIGHT

EASY

√324	√25	√324	√361	√144	√25	√49
√81	√400	√9	√256	√121	√100	√400
√441	√64	√1	√25	√196	√324	√676
√576	√529	√9	√196	√1	√441	√169
√196	√81	√25	√400	√441	√4	√9
√1	√121	√361	√144	√169	√484	√361
√25	√4	√225	√324	√36	√81	√9

WORDS

1. EATER
2. MUNCH
3. STABS
4. TRUNKS

EASY

√100	√9	√64	√256	√441	√400	√625
√529	√676	√576	√361	√64	√361	√81
√9	√25	√121	√400	√121	√81	√100
√1	√625	√144	√64	√9	√196	√4
√36	√400	√144	√81	√121	√81	√25
√625	√49	√324	√225	√484	√144	√361
√324	√361	√144	√16	√25	√16	√4

WORDS

1. VOLLEY
2. SICKLE
3. THIRTY
4. SINKS

EASY

√1	√144	√441	√1	√400	√196	√361
√25	√484	√400	√289	√81	√529	√64
√576	√9	√196	√529	√676	√1	√9
√121	√144	√1	√441	√225	√16	√169
√361	√25	√49	√324	√225	√196	√9
√4	√361	√16	√49	√81	√169	√49
√441	√400	√1	√625	√144	√441	√676

WORDS

1. SHADOW
2. GRACE
3. MOUNTAIN
4. SAYING

EASY

√1	√676	√361	√576	√4	√121	√100
√36	√81	√64	√441	√225	√100	√36
√324	√441	√324	√49	√256	√144	√121
√169	√1	√196	√1	√225	√361	√36
√324	√81	√361	√529	√400	√361	√25
√256	√25	√16	√25	√225	√361	√225
√121	√144	√81	√324	√324	√169	√16

WORDS

1. AFRAID
2. STORIES
3. FLOWERS
4. SUGAR

EASY

√529	√121	√100	√196	√49	√81	√9
√144	√441	√81	√441	√324	√49	√484
√324	√361	√225	√16	√400	√64	√324
√4	√529	√9	√144	√625	√361	√225
√324	√256	√225	√25	√4	√441	√9
√1	√9	√25	√64	√196	√16	√676
√441	√529	√625	√81	√49	√1	√16

WORDS

1. GROUND
2. COURTS
3. HOLDING
4. BRACE

EASY

√144	√1	√121	√625	√676	√529	√81
√9	√100	√324	√324	√144	√361	√169
√196	√36	√81	√144	√25	√4	√324
√121	√676	√16	√1	√4	√361	√289
√16	√225	√256	√441	√4	√16	√9
√25	√196	√324	√25	√196	√1	√4
√1	√16	√49	√81	√121	√144	√625

WORDS

1. BALLS
2. RUBBER
3. BANDS
4. ARIZONA

EASY

√16	√25	√256	√324	√676	√625	√484
√529	√81	√121	√1	√400	√81	√144
√169	√196	√169	√1	√121	√100	√81
√36	√676	√81	√361	√25	√25	√4
√1	√225	√25	√196	√121	√324	√49
√441	√361	√324	√361	√1	√144	√400
√484	√49	√25	√361	√361	√1	√484

WORDS

1. RAKES
2. FORSAKE
3. VITAMIN
4. GLASSES

EASY

√324	√121	√64	√25	√169	√484	√625
√529	√25	√625	√196	√529	√81	√225
√121	√400	√324	√81	√100	√529	√324
√16	√9	√196	√81	√64	√81	√81
√25	√256	√81	√1	√256	√400	√49
√289	√441	√64	√225	√144	√81	√400
√100	√169	√225	√36	√1	√196	√324

WORDS

1. POINTER
2. WITHIN
3. HAIRY
4. ORIGINAL

EASY

√256	√49	√324	√36	√25	√256	√361
√9	√324	√625	√400	√196	√441	√441
√361	√81	√400	√81	√100	√225	√1
√25	√400	√196	√49	√4	√25	√9
√400	√361	√81	√676	√81	√625	√529
√81	√1	√25	√64	√324	√36	√361
√100	√361	√400	√169	√225	√169	√196

WORDS

1. CITIES
2. ORIGIN
3. STATES
4. COUNTRY

EASY

√1	√25	√676	√625	√225	√25	√256
√441	√16	√400	√36	√400	√100	√25
√16	√400	√1	√81	√1	√25	√484
√49	√144	√25	√324	√441	√25	√64
√289	√1	√144	√9	√256	√81	√361
√361	√144	√324	√121	√144	√361	√441
√484	√289	√81	√4	√25	√9	√4

WORDS

1. FAUCET
2. SPRITE
3. SALAD
4. BELIEVE

EASY

√256	√49	√81	√49	√25	√25	√676
√625	√289	√9	√324	√25	√4	√196
√1	√16	√81	√196	√196	√256	√361
√324	√361	√9	√81	√64	√25	√121
√144	√225	√400	√100	√400	√196	√1
√324	√441	√25	√144	√225	√25	√289
√625	√529	√121	√81	√1	√441	√400

WORDS

1. ETHNIC
2. ROUTINE
3. ALONE
4. GREENS

EASY

√100	√144	√225	√121	√324	√64	√25
√256	√144	√441	√225	√196	√289	√484
√36	√324	√36	√324	√16	√25	√100
√400	√49	√16	√225	√361	√361	√25
√9	√16	√225	√196	√49	√484	√361
√81	√144	√121	√81	√225	√324	√256
√225	√81	√576	√676	√169	√400	√361

WORDS

1. GOODNESS
2. MINDFUL
3. FLOORS
4. STOVE

EASY

√225	√1	√289	√121	√256	√36	√256
√361	√529	√169	√676	√576	√64	√324
√81	√9	√1	√16	√36	√225	√25
√81	√676	√16	√169	√324	√81	√16
√196	√49	√361	√81	√324	√25	√441
√36	√49	√25	√256	√225	√9	√25
√400	√484	√81	√121	√16	√25	√144

WORDS

1. FRIDGE
2. DORMS
3. AMAZING
4. PRODUCE

EASY

√121	√16	√25	√676	√324	√64	√81
√289	√484	√441	√49	√81	√25	√1
√9	√196	√4	√441	√400	√196	√289
√225	√25	√324	√361	√196	√361	√256
√81	√196	√81	√225	√400	√1	√576
√16	√196	√324	√25	√121	√324	√144
√676	√361	√441	√36	√625	√81	√256

WORDS

1. FRIENDS
2. STRIKE
3. UNION
4. PLANNER

EASY

√441	√25	√64	√121	√144	√676	√625
√361	√25	√225	√16	√16	√256	√441
√400	√196	√25	√4	√289	√81	√324
√361	√576	√529	√4	√1	√9	√196
√16	√25	√81	√144	√121	√4	√49
√9	√324	√16	√81	√4	√81	√64
√36	√289	√169	√1	√324	√4	√196

WORDS

1. BLACK
2. RIBBONS
3. BRIDE
4. WEDDING

EASY

√9	√81	√441	√49	√121	√1	√9
√81	√400	√64	√4	√49	√144	√361
√625	√49	√324	√196	√625	√1	√25
√64	√529	√81	√361	√81	√25	√576
√49	√100	√169	√400	√16	√64	√144
√169	√676	√196	√1	√81	√361	√529
√625	√576	√144	√256	√169	√100	√1

WORDS

1. MIGHTY
2. SHINGLE
3. PANTS
4. IDEAS

EASY

√64	√121	√400	√1	√256	√484	√441
√324	√361	√4	√324	√625	√361	√144
√16	√1	√361	√676	√529	√1	√676
√25	√625	√25	√529	√169	√81	√49
√4	√1	√441	√49	√1	√196	√400
√100	√9	√81	√36	√1	√9	√4
√25	√256	√289	√324	√576	√529	√1

WORDS

1. WRAPS
2. BEARS
3. ANIMAL
4. CAGES

EASY

√121	√9	√441	√576	√121	√484	√400
√121	√144	√81	√16	√36	√144	√196
√169	√529	√144	√361	√36	√81	√25
√81	√9	√225	√256	√1	√1	√441
√576	√441	√4	√529	√225	√324	√9
√25	√4	√144	√225	√324	√36	√400
√361	√484	√9	√100	√121	√169	√81

WORDS

1. WAFFLE
2. LOOPS
3. CLICK
4. TRAIN

EASY

√144	√256	√25	√441	√529	√81	√64
√9	√100	√196	√9	√1	√121	√144
√324	√400	√484	√324	√324	√144	√324
√361	√225	√441	√1	√25	√529	√25
√36	√49	√400	√256	√144	√49	√144
√169	√100	√1	√81	√196	√36	√1
√4	√225	√36	√196	√289	√676	√625

WORDS

1. PERCENT
2. NATURAL
3. FLAVOR
4. FINGER

EASY

√121	√225	√25	√36	√144	√144	√441
√484	√289	√324	√25	√81	√225	√100
√36	√400	√25	√256	√64	√196	√196
√64	√121	√81	√169	√144	√49	√81
√4	√400	√484	√16	√441	√25	√625
√9	√441	√225	√25	√100	√676	√529
√1	√400	√441	√121	√324	√225	√484

WORDS

1. ACTIVE
2. WORKOUT
3. HOLLER
4. JUMPING

EASY

√256	√625	√144	√529	√81	√100	√121
√25	√400	√225	√25	√529	√4	√25
√25	√9	√16	√225	√81	√144	√1
√144	√4	√144	√361	√169	√121	√324
√361	√144	√25	√1	√196	√1	√36
√256	√25	√196	√16	√169	√441	√100
√400	√441	√324	√4	√484	√289	√121

WORDS

1. WOODS
2. UMBRELLA
3. ANKLE
4. BEETLE

EASY

√64	√676	√26	√324	√25	√100	√25
√144	√9	√1	√324	√400	√144	√361
√1	√81	√625	√400	√400	√81	√9
√4	√16	√256	√100	√289	√144	√49
√324	√169	√361	√1	√676	√625	√9
√529	√441	√121	√49	√64	√256	√225
√4	√529	√484	√25	√25	√9	√676

WORDS

1. BUMPY
2. CHEEKS
3. LITER
4. CATTLE

EASY

$\sqrt{100}$	$\sqrt{81}$	$\sqrt{256}$	$\sqrt{225}$	$\sqrt{361}$	$\sqrt{441}$	$\sqrt{484}$
$\sqrt{9}$	$\sqrt{4}$	$\sqrt{361}$	$\sqrt{49}$	$\sqrt{81}$	$\sqrt{64}$	$\sqrt{225}$
$\sqrt{144}$	$\sqrt{25}$	$\sqrt{144}$	$\sqrt{25}$	$\sqrt{144}$	$\sqrt{169}$	$\sqrt{16}$
$\sqrt{196}$	$\sqrt{25}$	$\sqrt{400}$	$\sqrt{400}$	$\sqrt{289}$	$\sqrt{196}$	$\sqrt{441}$
$\sqrt{196}$	$\sqrt{1}$	$\sqrt{81}$	$\sqrt{400}$	$\sqrt{441}$	$\sqrt{625}$	$\sqrt{49}$
$\sqrt{16}$	$\sqrt{4}$	$\sqrt{64}$	$\sqrt{225}$	$\sqrt{81}$	$\sqrt{529}$	$\sqrt{576}$
$\sqrt{289}$	$\sqrt{144}$	$\sqrt{9}$	$\sqrt{361}$	$\sqrt{144}$	$\sqrt{100}$	$\sqrt{400}$

WORDS

1. LITTLE
2. CHANNEL
3. SOUND
4. BITES

EASY

√361	√64	√289	√64	√196	√196	√121
√1	√144	√196	√25	√9	√225	√361
√4	√25	√1	√81	√400	√36	√81
√289	√676	√36	√324	√529	√81	√400
√676	√576	√36	√441	√576	√9	√121
√16	√121	√144	√441	√169	√225	√1
√256	√289	√256	√441	√484	√9	√4

WORDS

1. MUFFIN
2. KITCHEN
3. PLURALS
4. ACTIONS

EASY

√361	√256	√81	√9	√121	√100	√1
√576	√196	√529	√169	√529	√324	√196
√324	√441	√324	√225	√1	√361	√25
√400	√529	√441	√144	√196	√676	√121
√576	√4	√16	√361	√144	√9	√196
√4	√1	√625	√25	√81	√225	√81
√144	√196	√121	√256	√225	√256	√625

WORDS

1. MANSION
2. YELLOW
3. PICKER
4. BURNS

EASY

√256	√121	√100	√576	√16	√25	√529
√81	√9	√324	√81	√9	√81	√4
√256	√25	√144	√441	√196	√361	√36
√324	√49	√9	√121	√400	√25	√256
√196	√25	√25	√1	√441	√81	√529
√324	√1	√441	√361	√484	√225	√400
√4	√9	√25	√324	√361	√64	√9

WORDS

1. PENCIL
2. SECURE
3. OUTSIDE
4. RANGER

EASY

√144	√25	√361	√25	√121	√256	√441
√324	√484	√64	√361	√49	√196	√9
√4	√400	√1	√361	√225	√529	√625
√625	√49	√1	√81	√121	√64	√81
√9	√100	√25	√400	√324	√400	√144
√196	√529	√169	√1	√1	√100	√361
√81	√676	√625	√256	√324	√36	√49

WORDS

1. PARKS
2. GASES
3. STATION
4. WEATHER

EASY

√16	√225	√324	√49	√81	√121	√100
√144	√400	√64	√361	√441	√49	√81
√169	√4	√16	√144	√25	√225	√1
√256	√324	√361	√25	√169	√196	√289
√64	√1	√25	√4	√49	√81	√25
√16	√576	√529	√324	√9	√144	√361
√256	√144	√25	√196	√9	√81	√169

WORDS

1. ANGEL
2. WARMTH
3. CLIMBS
4. EXERCISE

EASY

√225	√576	√676	√64	√81	√4	√1
√4	√441	√25	√36	√144	√25	√256
√1	√121	√361	√16	√289	√484	√400
√441	√81	√25	√1	√4	√25	√64
√81	√9	√144	√324	√324	√1	√144
√36	√1	√25	√529	√9	√4	√625
√676	√576	√81	√121	√144	√1	√16

WORDS

1. VERBAL
2. ABUSE
3. ALIKE
4. CRADLE

EASY

√121	√256	√64	√1	√49	√81	√100
√121	√25	√169	√81	√225	√144	√324
√361	√196	√361	√441	√400	√484	√1
√676	√16	√1	√625	√9	√441	√441
√529	√196	√4	√64	√169	√81	√400
√121	√144	√441	√36	√400	√484	√100
√576	√289	√361	√324	√4	√9	√25

WORDS

1. MUTUAL
2. BANKS
3. FUNDS
4. VICTIM

EASY

√121	√36	√256	√100	√441	√484	√9
√16	√64	√400	√81	√25	√64	√361
√9	√144	√121	√441	√196	√196	√169
√676	√64	√9	√225	√81	√49	√625
√529	√1	√400	√1	√361	√576	√64
√4	√169	√484	√324	√1	√25	√16
√256	√225	√361	√100	√121	√441	√400

WORDS

1. VAINS
2. BACKING
3. EARTH
4. SOUTH

EASY

√361	√1	√196	√225	√25	√64	√100
√121	√144	√25	√400	√441	√81	√196
√484	√225	√169	√400	√49	√676	√81
√64	√529	√324	√9	√16	√324	√1
√361	√144	√9	√169	√25	√81	√196
√289	√324	√121	√4	√484	√1	√361
√25	√4	√1	√256	√529	√625	√121

WORDS

1. MEANT
2. VIRGINIA
3. CROWS
4. BEAKS

EASY

√81	√256	√49	√121	√100	√441	√484
√49	√81	√121	√25	√25	√361	√49
√144	√256	√196	√144	√484	√196	√225
√324	√361	√529	√25	√121	√81	√625
√361	√441	√441	√9	√529	√25	√484
√289	√25	√4	√400	√81	√529	√100
√4	√256	√64	√361	√1	√9	√16

WORDS

1. SEVEN
2. TIEING
3. BUCKLE
4. WASHES

EASY

√576	√484	√256	√121	√169	√625	√676
√64	√81	√1	√9	√400	√25	√16
√361	√49	√9	√64	√441	√1	√144
√441	√484	√196	√49	√441	√4	√625
√529	√400	√81	√169	√441	√225	√64
√81	√324	√64	√225	√324	√9	√4
√49	√25	√81	√1	√255	√256	√324

WORDS

1. VACUUM
2. THOUGHT
3. PROBLEM
4. AIRINGS

EASY

$\sqrt{361}$	$\sqrt{256}$	$\sqrt{625}$	$\sqrt{289}$	$\sqrt{1}$	$\sqrt{676}$	$\sqrt{625}$
$\sqrt{529}$	$\sqrt{81}$	$\sqrt{441}$	$\sqrt{196}$	$\sqrt{121}$	$\sqrt{256}$	$\sqrt{484}$
$\sqrt{441}$	$\sqrt{225}$	$\sqrt{400}$	$\sqrt{9}$	$\sqrt{169}$	$\sqrt{1}$	$\sqrt{144}$
$\sqrt{169}$	$\sqrt{81}$	$\sqrt{1}$	$\sqrt{225}$	$\sqrt{225}$	$\sqrt{49}$	$\sqrt{625}$
$\sqrt{4}$	$\sqrt{256}$	$\sqrt{441}$	$\sqrt{49}$	$\sqrt{9}$	$\sqrt{676}$	$\sqrt{25}$
$\sqrt{9}$	$\sqrt{9}$	$\sqrt{36}$	$\sqrt{64}$	$\sqrt{9}$	$\sqrt{1}$	$\sqrt{64}$
$\sqrt{64}$	$\sqrt{625}$	$\sqrt{676}$	$\sqrt{676}$	$\sqrt{324}$	$\sqrt{9}$	$\sqrt{529}$

WORDS

1. TOUCH
2. PACKAGE
3. CRAZY
4. COMPANY

EASY

√64	√625	√196	√9	√64	√225	√256
√144	√81	√1	√49	√4	√121	√1
√256	√121	√225	√324	√1	√36	√441
√1	√324	√361	√144	√676	√196	√400
√625	√400	√529	√25	√361	√289	√196
√625	√256	√400	√25	√441	√25	√100
√81	√64	√324	√25	√9	√441	√4

WORDS

1. BANQUET
2. ROACH
3. PRESENT
4. TAKING

EASY

√484	√144	√289	√676	√361	√400	√441
√484	√64	√81	√25	√16	√1	√9
√169	√400	√100	√400	√16	√676	√625
√625	√529	√16	√196	√196	√25	√4
√144	√81	√25	√225	√441	√1	√25
√361	√1	√9	√121	√361	√169	√625
√324	√25	√49	√25	√144	√49	√64

WORDS

1. SUNDAY
2. CONTEST
3. LEGAL
4. RESIDE

EASY

$\sqrt{25}$	$\sqrt{121}$	$\sqrt{25}$	$\sqrt{324}$	$\sqrt{361}$	$\sqrt{64}$	$\sqrt{576}$
$\sqrt{289}$	$\sqrt{196}$	$\sqrt{144}$	$\sqrt{256}$	$\sqrt{25}$	$\sqrt{121}$	$\sqrt{1}$
$\sqrt{4}$	$\sqrt{81}$	$\sqrt{25}$	$\sqrt{25}$	$\sqrt{324}$	$\sqrt{400}$	$\sqrt{361}$
$\sqrt{529}$	$\sqrt{196}$	$\sqrt{9}$	$\sqrt{529}$	$\sqrt{25}$	$\sqrt{400}$	$\sqrt{576}$
$\sqrt{25}$	$\sqrt{625}$	$\sqrt{81}$	$\sqrt{144}$	$\sqrt{625}$	$\sqrt{676}$	$\sqrt{25}$
$\sqrt{324}$	$\sqrt{36}$	$\sqrt{361}$	$\sqrt{16}$	$\sqrt{1}$	$\sqrt{49}$	$\sqrt{4}$
$\sqrt{9}$	$\sqrt{49}$	$\sqrt{100}$	$\sqrt{169}$	$\sqrt{25}$	$\sqrt{121}$	$\sqrt{324}$

WORDS

1. RENEW
2. BETTER
3. SLEEPS
4. MEDICINE

EASY

√144	√256	√225	√361	√484	√676	√625
√81	√9	√256	√324	√25	√196	√4
√25	√36	√16	√324	√225	√16	√25
√441	√196	√484	√25	√81	√324	√400
√81	√441	√9	√400	√256	√1	√4
√64	√169	√144	√1	√576	√1	√400
√324	√25	√361	√25	√196	√256	√100

WORDS

1. PREPARE
2. HUNDRED
3. NATION
4. TAXES

EASY

√676	√1	√64	√256	√121	√49	√81
√9	√25	√169	√1	√400	√4	√529
√9	√400	√144	√1	√49	√1	√121
√400	√225	√441	√25	√529	√144	√529
√25	√1	√361	√196	√625	√4	√9
√81	√100	√256	√25	√400	√225	√289
√324	√361	√441	√324	√361	√4	√1

WORDS

1. LAWYERS
2. ACCOUNT
3. WAGES
4. ATTEMPT

EASY

$\sqrt{100}$	$\sqrt{81}$	$\sqrt{4}$	$\sqrt{144}$	$\sqrt{196}$	$\sqrt{49}$	$\sqrt{9}$
$\sqrt{64}$	$\sqrt{25}$	$\sqrt{225}$	$\sqrt{81}$	$\sqrt{25}$	$\sqrt{361}$	$\sqrt{256}$
$\sqrt{324}$	$\sqrt{9}$	$\sqrt{441}$	$\sqrt{144}$	$\sqrt{196}$	$\sqrt{484}$	$\sqrt{400}$
$\sqrt{4}$	$\sqrt{400}$	$\sqrt{225}$	$\sqrt{441}$	$\sqrt{1}$	$\sqrt{676}$	$\sqrt{625}$
$\sqrt{529}$	$\sqrt{81}$	$\sqrt{196}$	$\sqrt{25}$	$\sqrt{81}$	$\sqrt{576}$	$\sqrt{25}$
$\sqrt{36}$	$\sqrt{64}$	$\sqrt{25}$	$\sqrt{16}$	$\sqrt{81}$	$\sqrt{144}$	$\sqrt{9}$
$\sqrt{361}$	$\sqrt{16}$	$\sqrt{1}$	$\sqrt{144}$	$\sqrt{16}$	$\sqrt{256}$	$\sqrt{441}$

WORDS

1. DIALING
2. COUNSEL
3. CLIENT
4. SHIELD

EASY

√324	√121	√144	√256	√676	√36	√529
√81	√9	√361	√49	√64	√36	√81
√196	√1	√196	√25	√4	√361	√25
√441	√49	√81	√484	√400	√225	√81
√484	√361	√81	√1	√144	√25	√144
√441	√361	√400	√169	√196	√324	√25
√225	√25	√1	√36	√324	√4	√9

WORDS

1. SOLVES
2. RETAIN
3. ASSIGN
4. BELIEF

EASY

√324	√169	√441	√484	√64	√121	√81
√676	√625	√324	√529	√576	√100	√196
√25	√625	√361	√1	√1	√441	√36
√25	√324	√1	√25	√144	√441	√324
√256	√64	√256	√81	√256	√289	√25
√144	√169	√196	√256	√400	√81	√9
√4	√16	√256	√1	√361	√625	√324

WORDS

1. PAYERS
2. QUALITY
3. APPEAR
4. INJURE

EASY

√25	√9	√1	√36	√144	√169	√81
√324	√196	√25	√196	√361	√196	√576
√529	√256	√1	√361	√441	√225	√361
√400	√576	√196	√25	√324	√81	√64
√484	√81	√25	√4	√361	√400	√9
√16	√289	√36	√625	√1	√676	√64
√81	√25	√361	√324	√225	√361	√441

WORDS

1. NORTH
2. EXPENSE
3. OASIS
4. FINANCE

EASY

√256	√1	√324	√676	√64	√81	√121
√144	√225	√256	√441	√625	√441	√400
√361	√9	√256	√144	√324	√25	√4
√625	√144	√16	√144	√361	√9	√49
√81	√100	√25	√361	√1	√324	√256
√169	√441	√676	√361	√25	√529	√441
√625	√64	√144	√121	√289	√100	√256

WORDS

1. APPLY
2. CASES
3. PURSE
4. JELLY

EASY

√289	√81	√121	√100	√25	√676	√625
√529	√361	√576	√144	√361	√4	√16
√100	√169	√64	√324	√121	√196	√441
√400	√4	√81	√1	√9	√81	√36
√9	√324	√400	√324	√529	√361	√400
√400	√441	√361	√1	√16	√4	√484
√121	√100	√1	√9	√256	√225	√324

WORDS

1. STARS
2. TICKLE
3. CARDS
4. SHIRT

EASY

√121	√100	√441	√484	√625	√529	√9
√49	√81	√1	√9	√16	√225	√1
√256	√64	√169	√289	√400	√529	√676
√324	√25	√625	√225	√196	√25	√625
√225	√9	√81	√196	√361	√441	√64
√400	√1	√225	√400	√529	√36	√81
√100	√529	√16	√81	√196	√49	√1

WORDS

1. AWESOME
2. FUNNY
3. WAITING
4. DOCTOR

EASY

√361	√144	√25	√400	√576	√1	√361
√225	√256	√225	√196	√196	√25	√16
√121	√100	√441	√196	√25	√324	√169
√144	√324	√25	√4	√441	√625	√81
√9	√400	√1	√49	√324	√400	√64
√25	√36	√1	√49	√225	√49	√100
√441	√484	√9	√25	√4	√16	√25

WORDS

1. ENTOURAGE
2. TUNNELS
3. CATEGORY
4. ADMIRE

EASY

√64	√625	√25	√256	√121	√144	√225
√1	√9	√36	√625	√4	√441	√676
√324	√1	√81	√529	√1	√625	√361
√169	√361	√625	√576	√529	√256	√676
√361	√81	√4	√9	√225	√4	√36
√1	√196	√9	√81	√324	√441	√25
√49	√144	√484	√256	√361	√9	√324

WORDS

1. FARMING
2. CROPS
3. CLASSIC
4. SUBWAY

EASY

$\sqrt{529}$	$\sqrt{576}$	$\sqrt{64}$	$\sqrt{121}$	$\sqrt{144}$	$\sqrt{324}$	$\sqrt{25}$
$\sqrt{441}$	$\sqrt{324}$	$\sqrt{100}$	$\sqrt{1}$	$\sqrt{121}$	$\sqrt{9}$	$\sqrt{441}$
$\sqrt{49}$	$\sqrt{25}$	$\sqrt{16}$	$\sqrt{225}$	$\sqrt{144}$	$\sqrt{81}$	$\sqrt{196}$
$\sqrt{484}$	$\sqrt{196}$	$\sqrt{81}$	$\sqrt{225}$	$\sqrt{1}$	$\sqrt{196}$	$\sqrt{1}$
$\sqrt{625}$	$\sqrt{529}$	$\sqrt{64}$	$\sqrt{9}$	$\sqrt{49}$	$\sqrt{16}$	$\sqrt{676}$
$\sqrt{529}$	$\sqrt{361}$	$\sqrt{81}$	$\sqrt{361}$	$\sqrt{529}$	$\sqrt{25}$	$\sqrt{1}$
$\sqrt{4}$	$\sqrt{9}$	$\sqrt{144}$	$\sqrt{25}$	$\sqrt{169}$	$\sqrt{196}$	$\sqrt{400}$

WORDS

1. HOOKING
2. ESCALADE
3. SWING
4. DANCER

EASY

√484	√121	√100	√81	√64	√484	√144
√625	√676	√4	√324	√25	√225	√4
√16	√25	√441	√144	√49	√529	√49
√36	√324	√324	√441	√25	√196	√81
√256	√144	√100	√324	√225	√81	√121
√324	√361	√36	√144	√4	√1	√49
√9	√25	√529	√64	√676	√625	√100

WORDS

1. BLOWER
2. FLOUR
3. GINGER
4. BLURP

EASY

√49	√256	√49	√81	√100	√121	√16
√81	√324	√529	√25	√625	√25	√676
√16	√36	√400	√144	√256	√361	√225
√1	√9	√49	√81	√4	√25	√49
√64	√529	√196	√49	√324	√484	√144
√361	√484	√49	√25	√441	√25	√25
√625	√529	√25	√361	√361	√100	√484

WORDS

1. GIFTING
2. JUGGLE
3. VESSEL
4. DESERVE

EASY

√121	√9	√64	√1	√256	√225	√625
√676	√441	√64	√400	√324	√484	√49
√81	√16	√25	√324	√25	√25	√144
√121	√9	√25	√16	√324	√64	√64
√36	√25	√400	√1	√676	√256	√400
√121	√169	√361	√361	√4	√361	√225
√676	√625	√529	√25	√81	√324	√4

WORDS

1. ERASE
2. CHECK
3. SISTER
4. BROTHER

EASY

√361	√1	√16	√144	√25	√256	√441
√400	√324	√144	√4	√9	√324	√484
√361	√4	√225	√81	√4	√25	√289
√484	√441	√196	√25	√4	√81	√36
√49	√256	√64	√225	√4	√324	√81
√676	√625	√441	√225	√529	√100	√16
√121	√144	√1	√9	√324	√81	√64

WORDS

1. HONORS
2. DRIBBLE
3. ROBBER
4. PUBLIC

EASY

√256	√48	√64	√100	√81	√225	√676
√625	√441	√64	√1	√4	√576	√529
√16	√49	√100	√225	√361	√289	√484
√169	√1	√441	√400	√324	√441	√400
√81	√64	√1	√361	√144	√324	√625
√625	√144	√676	√1	√25	√25	√4
√144	√169	√196	√25	√361	√400	√4

WORDS

1. MAJORS
2. BREAST
3. BELTS
4. LAUGH

EASY

√225	√64	√25	√100	√25	√81	√64
√81	√9	√256	√225	√400	√144	√196
√144	√361	√1	√144	√225	√144	√121
√256	√225	√49	√121	√256	√400	√441
√400	√64	√196	√81	√9	√484	√4
√625	√676	√225	√25	√196	√529	√576
√49	√400	√81	√25	√1	√9	√100

WORDS

1. POOPS
2. NECKLACE
3. TONIGHT
4. BULLETIN

EASY

√121	√1	√100	√144	√625	√441	√400
√81	√9	√36	√4	√225	√361	√16
√25	√256	√324	√225	√324	√196	√289
√49	√81	√484	√441	√1	√25	√121
√1	√9	√256	√196	√400	√529	√625
√676	√64	√169	√144	√25	√169	√16
√25	√1	√1	√49	√1	√36	√225

WORDS

1. AFRICA
2. TENORS
3. ALPHA
4. OMEGA

EASY

√400	√25	√256	√9	√100	√64	√81
√4	√196	√81	√1	√529	√441	√529
√576	√625	√324	√4	√81	√676	√441
√400	√484	√121	√81	√144	√484	√324
√169	√144	√25	√1	√196	√25	√25
√196	√49	√81	√484	√324	√49	√361
√100	√4	√9	√25	√400	√64	√121

WORDS

1. TRAVEL
2. WIVES
3. RINGER
4. CABINET

EASY

√256	√361	√4	√400	√25	√121	√64
√576	√625	√225	√1	√25	√256	√196
√1	√49	√25	√64	√361	√324	√9
√144	√121	√9	√16	√25	√36	√225
√100	√144	√25	√4	√1	√225	√169
√676	√625	√1	√144	√441	√324	√529
√576	√16	√25	√324	√361	√225	√256

WORDS

1. FOULED
2. BASEBALL
3. ARMOR
4. CHEETOS

ANSWERS

		√121=K (3)				
			√81=I (3)	√25=E (4)	√324=R (2)	
	√4=B (1)		√400=T (3)	√144=L (4)	√81=I (2)	
	√196=N (3)	√1=A (1)	√400=T (3)	√16=D (2)	√256=P (4)	
	√4=B (1)	√25=E (3)		√16=D (2)	√81=I (4)	
	√81=I (1)			√144=L (2)	√324=R (4)	
√25=E (1)	√361=S (1)		√25=E (2)			√400=T (4)

	√9=C (4)					
		√324=R (4)	√49=G (3)		√256=P (2)	
		√81=I (4)	√361=S (4)	√196=N (3)	√1=A (2)	
√25=E (2)	√64=H (1)	√441=U (2)	√4=B (4)	√324=R (2)	√81=I (3)	
	√400=T (2)	√1=A (1)	√64=H (2)	√1=A (2)	√49=G (3)	
		√196=N (1)	√25=E (1)	√9=C (2)		√1=A (3)
	√16=D (1)	√144=L (1)				

	√625=Y (2)				√361=S (4)	√9=C (3)
		√81=I (2)	√121=K (1)		√1=A (3)	√25=E (4)
		√25=E (2)	√196=N (1)		√196=N (3)	√144=L (4)
√16=D (2)	√144=L (2)	√225=O (1)		√49=G (1)	√4=B (4)	√9=C (3)
		√529=W (1)		√196=N (1)	√1=A (4)	√25=E (3)
			√81=I (1)	√9=C (4)	√324=R (3)	

						√49=G (1)
			√25=E (1)		√196=N (1)	√49=G (3)
√324=R (4)	√361=S (2)	√36=F (1)	√25=E (1)	√256=P (3)	√81=I (1)	√196=N (3)
√361=S (4)	√25=E (4)	√324=R (2)	√169=M (3)	√144=L (1)	√81=I (3)	
	√1=A (2)	√169=M (4)	√1=A (3)			
	√81=I (2)	√81=I (4)		√9=C (3)		
		√144=L (2)	√400=T (4)			

		√64=H (3)		√361=S (3)		
		√1=A (3)	√1=A (3)	√169=M (2)	√361=S (3)	√625=Y (4)
√361=S (2)		√324=R (3)		√81=I (2)	√256=P (4)	
	√324=R (2)	√16=D (1)	√196=N (2)	√256=P (4)	√25=E (1)	
		√225=O (2)	√225=O (1)	√1=A (4)	√144=L (1)	
			√441=U (1)	√4=B (1)	√64=H (4)	

	√144=L (3)	√25=E (3)				
		√1=A (3)		√361=S (2)		
		√324=R (3)	√81=I (2)	√324=R (4)		
√361=S (3)	√196=N (3)		√196=N (2)		√25=E (4)	√144=L (4)
	√144=L (1)		√49=G (2)	√196=N (1)	√25=E (4)	√400=T (4)
		√1=A (1)	√144=L (2)	√225=O (1)	√400=T (4)	
		√324=R (1)	√361=S (1)	√25=E (2)		

		$\sqrt{16}=D$ (4)				
		$\sqrt{25}=E$ (4)				
	$\sqrt{144}=L$ (4)	$\sqrt{225}=O$ (2)	$\sqrt{196}=N$ (3)	$\sqrt{400}=T$ (2)	$\sqrt{81}=I$ (2)	$\sqrt{324}=R$ (3)
$\sqrt{400}=T$ (4)	$\sqrt{25}=E$ (4)	$\sqrt{81}=I$ (3)	$\sqrt{441}=U$ (2)	$\sqrt{196}=N$ (3)	$\sqrt{25}=E$ (3)	$\sqrt{196}=N$ (2)
$\sqrt{25}=E$ (1)	$\sqrt{16}=D$ (3)				$\sqrt{25}=E$ (1)	$\sqrt{49}=G$ (2)
			$\sqrt{361}=S$ (1)	$\sqrt{361}=S$ (1)		
		$\sqrt{625}=Y$ (1)	$\sqrt{1}=A$ (1)			

		$\sqrt{400}=T$ (4)	$\sqrt{25}=E$ (4)			
	$\sqrt{1}=A$ (4)	$\sqrt{25}=E$ (1)	$\sqrt{324}=R$ (1)	$\sqrt{324}=R$ (4)		
	$\sqrt{144}=L$ (1)	$\sqrt{529}=W$ (4)	$\sqrt{400}=T$ (2)	$\sqrt{25}=E$ (1)	$\sqrt{361}=S$ (4)	
$\sqrt{625}=Y$ (1)		$\sqrt{25}=E$ (2)	$\sqrt{1}=A$ (2)	$\sqrt{169}=M$ (1)		
	$\sqrt{361}=S$ (3)		$\sqrt{144}=L$ (2)	$\sqrt{81}=I$ (3)	$\sqrt{400}=T$ (3)	$\sqrt{361}=S$ (3)
		$\sqrt{49}=G$ (3)	$\sqrt{196}=N$ (3)	$\sqrt{25}=E$ (2)		
				$\sqrt{324}=R$ (2)		

		√36=F (3)	√16=D (4)				
		√196=N (4)	√225=O (3)	√361=S (4)	√400=T (2)		
		√1=A (4)	√144=L (3)		√324=R (2)		
	√64=H (4)		√324=R (1)	√16=D (3)	√81=I (2)		
		√81=I (1)	√441=U (1)	√49=G (2)	√25=E (3)		
√361=S (2)	√324=R (2)	√196=N (1)	√49=G (2)	√225=O (1)		√324=R (3)	
		√25=E (2)	√49=G (1)	√256=P (1)			

		√81=I (1)	√169=M (1)				
		√9=C (1)	√625=Y (2)				
	√361=S (1)	√324=R (1)	√196=N (2)				
	√225=O (1)		√196=N (2)	√361=S (3)		√9=C (4)	
		√81=I (3)	√196=N (3)	√25=E (2)		√225=O (4)	
	√225=O (3)	√400=T (4)	√9=C (4)	√256=P (2)	√144=L (4)		
√9=C (3)				√25=E (4)	√144=L (4)		

		$\sqrt{361}$=S (2)			$\sqrt{16}$=D (3)	
		$\sqrt{1}$=A (2)			$\sqrt{25}$=E (1)	$\sqrt{324}$=R (3)
$\sqrt{361}$=S (4)			$\sqrt{36}$=F (2)	$\sqrt{9}$=C (1)	$\sqrt{1}$=A (3)	$\sqrt{361}$=S (1)
	$\sqrt{1}$=A (4)		$\sqrt{25}$=E (2)	$\sqrt{64}$=H (1)	$\sqrt{400}$=T (3)	$\sqrt{225}$=O (1)
		$\sqrt{196}$=N (4)	$\sqrt{400}$=T (2)	$\sqrt{361}$=S (3)	$\sqrt{225}$=O (1)	
	$\sqrt{16}$=D (4)	$\sqrt{169}$=M (3)	$\sqrt{441}$=U (3)	$\sqrt{625}$=Y (2)		

$\sqrt{441}$=U (2)				$\sqrt{196}$=N (4)		
$\sqrt{196}$=N (2)			$\sqrt{81}$=I (4)	$\sqrt{49}$=G (4)	$\sqrt{361}$=S (1)	
	$\sqrt{16}$=D (2)		$\sqrt{121}$=K (4)		$\sqrt{1}$=A (1)	$\sqrt{49}$=G (3)
	$\sqrt{25}$=E (2)	$\sqrt{81}$=I (4)		$\sqrt{36}$=F (3)	$\sqrt{196}$=N (1)	$\sqrt{196}$=N (3)
	$\sqrt{4}$=B (4)	$\sqrt{324}$=R (2)	$\sqrt{225}$=O (3)	$\sqrt{16}$=D (1)	$\sqrt{81}$=I (3)	
		$\sqrt{225}$=O (3)		$\sqrt{144}$=L (1)		
		$\sqrt{324}$=R (3)			$\sqrt{25}$=E (1)	

		√49=G (3)			
	√196=N (3)	√16=D (1)	√144=L (1)		√324=R (4)
	√144=L (1)	√81=I (3)	√625=Y (1)	√25=E (4)	
√324=R (1)			√256=P (3)	√256=P (4)	√256=P (4)
	√225=O (1)	√81=I (2)	√225=O (3)	√9=C (2)	√81=I (4)
	√196=N (2)	√529=W (1)	√1=A (2)	√64=H (3)	√1=A (2)
			√400=T (2)	√256=P (2)	

					√361=S (4)	
				√400=T (4)	√25=E (4)	
			√49=G (1)		√324=R (3)	√16=D (4)
√4=B (2)	√324=R (2)	√196=N (1)	√49=G (2)	√25=E (4)	√144=L (4)	√25=E (3)
		√81=I (2)	√81=I (1)	√64=H (2)	√400=T (2)	√16=D (3)
			√16=D (1)		√225=O (3)	√144=L (3)
		√64=H (1)	√225=O (1)	√144=L (1)		

				√4=B (4)		
		√49=G (2)	√169=M (4)	√49=G (3)	√144=L (4)	√25=E (4)
	√64=H (1)	√441=U (4)	√196=N (2)	√196=N (3)	√625=Y (1)	
	√324=R (4)	√81=I (1)	√81=I (2)	√1=A (1)	√81=I (3)	
√9=C (4)		√49=G (1)	√484=V (2)	√529=W (1)	√225=O (3)	√16=D (3)
		√81=I (2)	√64=H (1)			
		√144=L (2)				

PAGE 22

				√16=D (4)		
		√256=P (4)	√529=W (4)		√25=E (4)	
√361=S (1)	√144=L (2)	√225=O (4)		√64=H (3)	√324=R (4)	√361=S (2)
√9=C (1)		√81=I (2)		√9=C (3)	√324=R (2)	
	√324=R (1)	√81=I (1)	√196=N (2)	√25=E (2)	√324=R (3)	
		√256=P (1)	√64=H (3)	√441=U (3)		
		√9=C (3)	√400=T (1)			

$\sqrt{36}=F$ (1)					$\sqrt{400}=T$ (2)	
	$\sqrt{225}=O$ (1)			$\sqrt{196}=N$ (2)		
	$\sqrt{196}=N$ (1)	$\sqrt{400}=T$ (1)	$\sqrt{361}=S$ (3)	$\sqrt{81}=I$ (2)		
	$\sqrt{361}=S$ (1)	$\sqrt{441}=U$ (3)		$\sqrt{64}=H$ (3)	$\sqrt{1}=A$ (2)	
		$\sqrt{324}=R$ (3)			$\sqrt{256}=P$ (2)	
	$\sqrt{361}=S$ (4)	$\sqrt{4}=B$ (3)			$\sqrt{441}=U$ (4)	$\sqrt{324}=R$ (4)
		$\sqrt{324}=R$ (4)	$\sqrt{25}=E$ (4)	$\sqrt{144}=L$ (4)		

		$\sqrt{1}=A$ (4)			$\sqrt{169}=M$ (1)	
$\sqrt{324}=R$ (2)			$\sqrt{196}=N$ (4)		$\sqrt{4}=B$ (1)	$\sqrt{441}=U$ (1)
	$\sqrt{81}=I$ (2)	$\sqrt{1}=A$ (4)	$\sqrt{25}=E$ (3)	$\sqrt{25}=E$ (1)		$\sqrt{196}=N$ (1)
	$\sqrt{1}=A$ (2)	$\sqrt{196}=N$ (4)	$\sqrt{144}=L$ (3)	$\sqrt{324}=R$ (1)		
	$\sqrt{1}=A$ (4)	$\sqrt{256}=P$ (2)	$\sqrt{361}=S$ (1)	$\sqrt{256}=P$ (3)		
	$\sqrt{4}=B$ (4)			$\sqrt{169}=M$ (3)		
					$\sqrt{1}=A$ (3)	

						$\sqrt{25}$=E (4)	
					$\sqrt{361}$=S (2)	$\sqrt{144}$=L (4)	$\sqrt{361}$=S (4)
		$\sqrt{169}$=M (1)	$\sqrt{256}$=P (1)	$\sqrt{324}$=R (2)		$\sqrt{361}$=S (4)	$\sqrt{4}$=B (4)
		$\sqrt{1}$=A (1)	$\sqrt{25}$=E (2)	$\sqrt{81}$=I (1)			$\sqrt{225}$=O (4)
$\sqrt{49}$=G (3)	$\sqrt{144}$=L (3)	$\sqrt{64}$=H (1)	$\sqrt{9}$=C (2)	$\sqrt{225}$=O (1)	$\sqrt{100}$=J (4)		
$\sqrt{196}$=N (3)	$\sqrt{9}$=C (1)	$\sqrt{225}$=O (3)	$\sqrt{1}$=A (2)			$\sqrt{196}$=N (1)	
	$\sqrt{81}$=I (3)	$\sqrt{484}$=V (3)	$\sqrt{256}$=P (2)				

$\sqrt{441}$=U (4)	$\sqrt{25}$=E (4)			$\sqrt{169}$=M (1)		
	$\sqrt{400}$=T (4)	$\sqrt{4}$=B (3)	$\sqrt{1}$=A (1)			
	$\sqrt{324}$=R (4)	$\sqrt{324}$=R (3)	$\sqrt{25}$=E (1)	$\sqrt{196}$=N (3)	$\sqrt{9}$=C (3)	
		$\sqrt{81}$=I (4)	$\sqrt{1}$=A (3)	$\sqrt{324}$=R (1)		$\sqrt{64}$=H (3)
	$\sqrt{484}$=V (4)		$\sqrt{400}$=T (2)	$\sqrt{9}$=C (1)		
	$\sqrt{16}$=D (2)	$\sqrt{25}$=E (2)	$\sqrt{144}$=L (2)	$\sqrt{64}$=H (2)		
			$\sqrt{49}$=G (2)	$\sqrt{81}$=I (2)		

			√49=G (2)			
				√196=N (2)		
			√484=V (1)	√81=I (2)		
√361=S (4)	√25=E (4)	√169=M (2)	√169=M (2)	√1=A (1)		
	√576=X (4)	√441=U (2)	√4=B (4)		√144=L (1)	
	√64=H (2)	√225=O (4)	√324=R (3)	√81=I (3)	√441=U (1)	√25=E (1)
			√49=G (3)	√16=D (3)	√361=S (3)	

			√9=C (2)			
		√1=A (4)	√64=H (2)			
	√400=T (4)	√81=I (2)	√144=L (4)	√196=N (1)		√49=G (3)
	√196=N (4)	√144=L (2)		√81=I (1)	√49=G (1)	√196=N (3)
√25=E (4)	√36=F (1)		√16=D (2)	√400=T (1)	√81=I (3)	
	√169=M (4)	√1=A (1)	√361=S (1)	√400=T (3)		
			√361=S (3)	√1=A (3)	√144=L (3)	

			$\sqrt{225}$=O (3)			
				$\sqrt{400}$=T (3)		
$\sqrt{49}$=G (2)	$\sqrt{36}$=F (2)		$\sqrt{324}$=R (3)	$\sqrt{64}$=H (3)	$\sqrt{144}$=L (4)	
$\sqrt{196}$=N (2)	$\sqrt{81}$=I (2)	$\sqrt{361}$=S (3)	$\sqrt{361}$=S (1)	$\sqrt{25}$=E (3)	$\sqrt{16}$=D (4)	$\sqrt{25}$=E (4)
$\sqrt{196}$=N (2)	$\sqrt{81}$=I (2)		$\sqrt{81}$=I (1)	$\sqrt{361}$=S (1)	$\sqrt{1}$=A (1)	$\sqrt{196}$=N (4)
$\sqrt{16}$=D (2)		$\sqrt{196}$=N (1)	$\sqrt{49}$=G (1)	$\sqrt{9}$=C (4)	$\sqrt{1}$=A (4)	$\sqrt{256}$=P (1)

		$\sqrt{16}$=D (2)		$\sqrt{4}$=B (4)		
		$\sqrt{25}$=E (2)	$\sqrt{4}$=B (4)		$\sqrt{144}$=L (4)	$\sqrt{25}$=E (4)
		$\sqrt{225}$=O (4)	$\sqrt{81}$=I (2)	$\sqrt{625}$=Y (3)	$\sqrt{9}$=C (2)	
		$\sqrt{4}$=B (4)	$\sqrt{324}$=R (2)	$\sqrt{144}$=L (3)	$\sqrt{1}$=A (2)	
		$\sqrt{64}$=H (1)	$\sqrt{81}$=I (3)	$\sqrt{324}$=R (2)		
	$\sqrt{361}$=S (1)	$\sqrt{1}$=A (1)	$\sqrt{400}$=T (1)	$\sqrt{1}$=A (3)		
$\sqrt{121}$=K (1)	$\sqrt{196}$=N (1)			$\sqrt{16}$=D (3)		

						√25=E (3)
	√25=E (4)		√144=L (1)		√169=M (3)	√16=D (3)
	√144=L (4)	√9=C (1)	√1=A (1)	√324=R (3)		
√256=P (4)	√9=C (2)	√64=H (2)	√225=O (3)	√361=S (1)		
√81=I (4)	√1=A (2)	√361=S (4)	√36=F (3)	√64=H (1)		
	√9=C (4)	√25=E (2)	√81=I (4)	√196=N (3)		
		√400=T (2)	√16=D (4)	√81=I (3)		

				√144=L (4)		
	√49=G (1)	√324=R (2)	√81=I (1)	√25=E (3)	√1=A (4)	
	√25=E (2)	√196=N (1)	√400=T (3)	√121=K (1)	√25=E (4)	
		√16=D (2)	√441=U (3)	√324=R (1)		√324=R (4)
	√169=M (3)	√256=P (3)	√196=N (2)	√1=A (1)		
	√225=O (3)		√169=M (1)	√81=I (2)	√4=B (2)	
√9=C (3)						

		√196=N (1)	√49=G (1)	√324=R (2)		
		√81=I (1)	√361=S (4)		√25=E (2)	
		√441=U (4)	√49=G (1)	√64=H (4)	√400=T (2)	√361=S (4)
	√256=P (4)		√49=G (1)	√64=H (2)	√25=E (4)	
		√441=U (3)	√1=A (1)	√49=G (2)		
	√4=B (3)	√4=B (1)	√400=T (3)	√81=I (2)	√144=L (2)	
√196=N (3)	√225=O (3)	√400=T (3)				

				√324=R (2)		
			√25=E (2)	√361=S (3)		
	√361=S (1)	√400=T (2)			√324=R (3)	
	√324=R (1)	√324=R (2)	√1=A (1)		√25=E (3)	
	√1=A (2)	√25=E (1)	√625=Y (1)	√144=L (1)	√256=P (1)	√529=W (3)
√121=K (4)	√400=T (2)	√225=O (4)	√144=L (4)	√400=T (4)	√441=U (4)	√225=O (3)
	√225=O (4)	√361=S (2)			√256=P (3)	√225=O (4)

			√196=N (3)			
	√4=B (2)		√121=K (3)	√81=I (3)	√324=R (3)	
		√144=L (2)			√25=E (4)	√16=D (3)
		√25=E (2)	√9=C (1)		√49=G (4)	
	√361=S (2)			√64=H (1)	√324=R (1)	√25=E (4)
√361=S (2)			√400=T (1)	√225=O (4)	√81=I (1)	√144=L (4)
			√9=C (4)	√361=S (1)	√144=L (4)	

	√361=S (4)	√400=T (4)				
		√361=S (1)	√225=O (4)		√25=E (4)	√25=E (3)
		√400=T (2)	√441=U (1)	√324=R (4)	√1=A (3)	√361=S (4)
		√256=P (1)	√324=R (2)	√1=A (2)	√324=R (3)	
		√169=M (1)		√25=E (2)	√324=R (3)	
	√1=A (1)	√49=G (3)	√196=N (3)	√81=I (3)	√64=H (2)	
√9=C (1)						

				√196=N (2)	√81=I (2)	
	√4=B (1)			√49=G (2)	√144=L (2)	√25=E (4)
		√225=O (1)		√324=R (2)	√400=T (4)	√324=R (4)
		√441=U (1)	√25=E (3)	√25=E (2)	√196=N (4)	
	√49=G (1)		√144=L (3)	√441=U (4)	√400=T (2)	
	√64=H (1)	√4=B (3)	√1=A (3)	√225=O (4)	√361=S (2)	
√400=T (1)			√400=T (3)		√9=C (4)	

				√324=R (1)		
				√225=O (1)		
				√25=E (2)	√9=C (1)	
	√256=P (3)	√441=U (3)	√196=N (1)	√9=C (2)	√121=K (1)	
√25=E (4)	√16=D (4)	√49=G (1)	√16=D (3)	√81=I (1)	√81=I (2)	
	√25=E (3)	√81=I (4)	√16=D (3)	√81=I (4)	√529=W (2)	
		√144=L (3)	√361=S (4)	√196=N (4)		√400=T (2)

		√361=S (1)	√25=E (1)			
√49=G (3)			√361=S (1)	√361=S (1)		
√196=N (3)				√25=E (1)	√49=G (2)	√529=W (4)
√81=I (3)	√400=T (2)			√324=R (1)	√196=N (2)	√25=E (4)
	√324=R (3)	√1=A (2)	√121=K (2)	√81=I (2)	√16=D (1)	√324=R (4)
		√1=A (3)			√9=C (4)	
			√9=C (3)		√361=S (4)	

PAGE 40

		√25=E (2)				
		√144=L (2)	√25=E (1)	√196=N (1)	√400=T (4)	
		√529=W (1)	√49=G (2)	√400=T (1)	√361=S (4)	
		√400=T (1)	√49=G (2)	√441=U (4)	√625=Y (1)	
	√25=E (3)	√121=K (3)	√225=O (2)	√324=R (3)	√324=R (4)	
√25=E (3)			√25=E (3)	√49=G (2)		√400=T (4)
√361=S (3)						

√25=E (3)				√225=O (1)		
	√324=R (3)		√144=L (1)	√324=R (2)	√529=W (1)	√361=S (4)
		√1=A (3)	√144=L (1)		√25=E (2)	√400=T (4)
	√144=L (2)	√441=U (3)	√225=O (1)	√16=D (2)	√225=O (4)	
	√289=Q (3)	√25=E (2)	√1=A (2)	√36=F (1)	√225=O (4)	
		√361=S (3)				√324=R (4)

					√196=N (4)	
			√144=L (2)		√81=I (4)	√49=G (4)
	√256=P (3)		√144=L (2)	√625=Y (2)	√25=E (4)	
	√25=E (3)	√324=R (1)	√25=E (1)	√1=A (2)	√529=W (1)	√25=E (4)
		√1=A (3)	√196=N (1)	√400=T (2)	√81=I (1)	√361=S (4)
	√9=C (3)	√400=T (2)	√225=O (2)	√196=N (1)		
√25=E (3)						

			√144=L (4)	√49=G (3)		
		√484=V (4)	√196=N (3)	√25=E (4)		
		√25=E (4)	√81=I (3)	√324=R (1)	√64=H (4)	√361=S (4)
	√81=I (2)	√361=S (4)	√1=A (1)	√361=S (3)	√441=U (3)	√64=H (3)
		√9=C (2)	√25=E (1)		√225=O (3)	
	√196=N (2)	√81=I (2)		√144=L (1)		
√49=G (2)				√9=C (1)		

	√361=S (2)				√64=H (1)	
	√121=K (4)	√64=H (2)	√49=G (3)	√1=A (3)	√1=A (1)	
√361=S (4)	√9=C (4)	√25=E (2)	√25=E (3)	√324=R (1)	√169=M (3)	
	√16=D (2)	√1=A (4)	√324=R (1)	√4=B (1)	√1=A (3)	
	√361=S (2)		√324=R (4)	√225=O (1)		√16=D (3)
			√9=C (4)			

PAGE 45

		√324=R (1)	√400=T (2)			
√361=S (3)		√324=R (2)	√25=E (1)			√324=R (4)
	√441=U (3)	√25=E (2)	√256=P (1)		√441=U (4)	
	√225=O (3)	√169=M (1)	√361=S (2)	√9=C (4)		
√625=Y (3)	√16=D (1)	√1=A (1)		√196=N (2)	√9=C (4)	
	√225=O (3)			√81=I (2)	√225=O (4)	
	√100=J (3)					

PAGE 46

		√49=G (3)		√225=O (4)	√36=F (1)	
	√361=S (2)	√196=N (3)		√36=F (4)	√81=I (1)	
√256=P (2)		√81=I (3)		√36=F (1)	√36=F (4)	
√1=A (2)	√625=Y (3)	√9=C (2)		√400=T (1)		√81=I (4)
	√144=L (2)	√441=U (3)	√4=B (3)		√625=Y (1)	√9=C (4)
					√25=E (4)	

	√4=B (4)		√25=E (4)			
√324=R (4)		√361=S (4)	√196=N (1)	√144=L (3)		
√441=U (4)	√81=I (4)		√81=I (1)	√49=G (1)	√225=O (3)	
	√625=Y (2)	√144=L (1)	√196=N (2)		√64=H (3)	
	√25=E (2)	√81=I (1)	√400=T (2)	√25=E (2)	√4=B (2)	√225=O (3)
		√144=L (2)	√1=A (1)		√9=C (3)	
			√169=M (1)		√144=L (3)	√1=A (3)

PAGE 48

		√196=N (3)				
		√49=G (3)	√81=I (3)	√9=C (1)		
	√36=F (2)		√16=D (3)	√324=R (1)		
√49=G (2)		√81=I (2)	√441=U (1)	√1=A (3)	√25=E (3)	√64=H (3)
√196=N (2)		√144=L (2)	√81=I (1)			
	√81=I (2)	√144=L (4)	√25=E (4)	√361=S (1)	√25=E (1)	
	√361=S (4)			√4=B (4)	√1=A (4)	√144=L (4)

					$\sqrt{49}=G$ (4)	
	$\sqrt{25}=E$ (1)				$\sqrt{225}=O$ (4)	
$\sqrt{361}=S$ (2)	$\sqrt{64}=H$ (1)	$\sqrt{324}=R$ (1)		$\sqrt{25}=E$ (3)		$\sqrt{81}=I$ (4)
$\sqrt{361}=S$ (1)	$\sqrt{196}=N$ (2)	$\sqrt{361}=S$ (1)	$\sqrt{256}=P$ (3)		$\sqrt{16}=D$ (3)	$\sqrt{196}=N$ (4)
$\sqrt{441}=U$ (1)		$\sqrt{1}=A$ (2)	$\sqrt{144}=L$ (3)		$\sqrt{49}=G$ (4)	
	$\sqrt{64}=H$ (3)	$\sqrt{25}=E$ (3)	$\sqrt{324}=R$ (2)	$\sqrt{400}=T$ (2)		

			$\sqrt{9}=C$ (3)			
	$\sqrt{4}=B$ (4)		$\sqrt{1}=A$ (4)	$\sqrt{64}=H$ (3)		
		$\sqrt{225}=O$ (4)	$\sqrt{324}=R$ (4)	$\sqrt{1}=A$ (3)		$\sqrt{49}=G$ (2)
$\sqrt{64}=H$ (1)		$\sqrt{324}=R$ (1)	$\sqrt{81}=I$ (3)	$\sqrt{16}=D$ (4)	$\sqrt{25}=E$ (2)	
	$\sqrt{400}=T$ (1)	$\sqrt{324}=R$ (3)	$\sqrt{441}=U$ (1)	$\sqrt{121}=K$ (2)	$\sqrt{25}=E$ (2)	
		$\sqrt{361}=S$ (3)	$\sqrt{361}=S$ (2)	$\sqrt{225}=O$ (1)		
			$\sqrt{36}=F$ (1)			

		√196=N (3)	√49=G (3)			
		√16=D (1)	√81=I (3)			√361=S (3)
	√25=E (1)		√9=C (2)	√196=N (3)	√81=I (3)	
√324=R (1)		√25=E (2)	√81=I (2)	√36=F (1)	√196=N (3)	√25=E (4)
	√25=E (1)	√256=P (4)	√1=A (1)	√324=R (2)	√9=C (4)	
	√324=R (4)	√64=H (1)	√400=T (1)	√81=I (4)	√256=P (2)	
	√1=A (4)	√9=C (4)	√400=T (4)			

PAGE 52

√25=E (1)						
	√144=L (1)		√625=Y (2)	√25=E (3)		
	√256=P (1)	√1=A (1)	√361=S (3)	√324=R (2)	√64=H (3)	
		√400=T (3)	√400=T (1)	√225=O (2)	√49=G (3)	
			√361=S (1)	√81=I (3)	√144=L (2)	
	√9=C (4)		√144=L (4)	√64=H (3)	√49=G (2)	√49=G (4)
		√25=E (4)	√81=I (4)	√81=I (4)	√196=N (4)	

						√361=S (4)
			√225=O (1)	√144=L (2)	√16=D (4)	
		√144=L (1)	√256=P (2)	√225=O (1)	√25=E (2)	√1=A (4)
	√225=O (2)	√441=U (2)	√25=E (3)	√64=H (1)		√25=E (4)
√9=C (2)	√196=N (3)	√16=D (3)	√9=C (1)	√324=R (3)	√324=R (4)	
	√225=O (3)		√361=S (1)		√4=B (4)	
	√529=W (3)					

		√484=V (4)				
	√144=L (4)	√25=E (4)	√81=I (4)		√625=Y (1)	
√361=S (4)	√400=T (4)	√225=O (4)	√324=R (2)	√441=U (3)	√400=T (1)	√361=S (3)
		√25=E (2)	√225=O (3)	√81=I (1)	√256=P (3)	√49=G (2)
		√1=A (2)	√324=R (3)	√144=L (1)	√196=N (2)	
		√49=G (3)	√16=D (2)	√81=I (2)	√81=I (1)	√1=A (1)
						√4=B (1)

		√361=S (1)			√49=G (3)	
	√625=Y (2)	√81=I (1)			√1=A (3)	
	√324=R (2)	√144=L (1)	√9=C (2)	√25=E (1)	√144=L (3)	
√361=S (4)	√400=T (4)	√441=U (2)	√484=V (1)	√324=R (2)	√324=R (1)	√1=A (3)
		√25=E (4)	√196=N (4)	√25=E (2)	√144=L (4)	√576=X (3)
			√169=M (2)	√1=A (4)	√625=Y (3)	√256=P (4)

√121=K (1)				√196=N (4)		
	√9=C (1)		√361=S (2)	√49=G (4)	√81=I (4)	
	√225=O (1)	√49=G (2)	√1=A (3)	√196=N (3)	√361=S (4)	
	√196=N (1)	√484=V (3)	√196=N (2)	√361=S (4)	√9=C (3)	
	√16=D (3)	√121=K (1)	√1=A (2)	√225=O (4)	√25=E (3)	
		√1=A (3)		√49=G (2)	√324=R (4)	
						√9=C (4)

		√529=W (3)				√400=T (4)
		√324=R (3)			√64=H (4)	
	√225=O (3)				√4=B (2)	√49=G (4)
	√196=N (3)	√121=K (1)	√144=L (1)	√1=A (2)	√144=L (2)	√81=I (4)
√49=G (3)		√25=E (1)	√9=C (2)	√1=A (1)	√25=E (2)	√324=R (4)
	√324=R (1)		√64=H (2)	√529=W (1)		

PAGE 58

√324=R (1)	√25=E (1)		√361=S (4)			
	√400=T (1)			√121=K (4)		√400=T (4)
	√64=H (2)	√1=A (1)	√25=E (1)	√196=N (4)	√324=R (4)	
		√9=C (2)	√196=N (2)	√1=A (3)	√441=U (4)	
			√400=T (3)	√441=U (2)	√4=B (3)	
		√361=S (3)		√169=M (2)		√361=S (3)

			√361=S (4)		√361=S (2)	
	√25=E (1)		√400=T (3)	√121=K (4)	√81=I (2)	
	√625=Y (1)	√144=L (1)	√64=H (3)	√9=C (2)	√196=N (4)	
	√400=T (3)	√144=L (1)	√81=I (3)	√121=K (2)	√81=I (4)	
√625=Y (3)		√324=R (3)	√225=O (1)	√484=V (1)	√144=L (2)	√361=S (4)
				√25=E (2)		

			√1=A (3)		√196=N (3)	√361=S (1)
√25=E (2)		√400=T (3)		√81=I (3)		√64=H (1)
	√9=C (2)	√196=N (3)	√529=W (1)		√1=A (1)	
		√1=A (2)	√441=U (3)	√225=O (1)	√16=D (1)	
			√324=R (2)	√225=O (3)	√196=N (4)	
	√361=S (4)		√49=G (2)	√81=I (4)	√169=M (3)	√49=G (4)
		√1=A (4)	√625=Y (4)			

PAGE 61

√1=A (1)		√361=S (4)				
√36=F (1)			√441=U (4)			√36=F (3)
√324=R (1)		√324=R (4)	√49=G (4)		√144=L (3)	
	√1=A (1)		√1=A (4)	√225=O (3)	√361=S (2)	
	√81=I (1)	√361=S (2)	√529=W (3)	√400=T (2)		
	√25=E (2)	√16=D (1)	√25=E (3)	√225=O (2)	√361=S (3)	
		√81=I (2)	√324=R (2)	√324=R (3)		

PAGE 62

			√196=N (3)	√49=G (3)		
		√81=I (3)	√441=U (2)	√324=R (2)	√49=G (1)	
		√225=O (2)	√16=D (3)	√400=T (2)		√324=R (1)
√4=B (4)		√9=C (2)	√144=L (3)		√361=S (2)	√225=O (1)
√324=R (4)		√225=O (3)			√441=U (1)	
√1=A (4)	√9=C (4)	√25=E (4)	√64=H (3)	√196=N (1)	√16=D (1)	

	√1=A (4)					
		√324=R (4)	√324=R (2)	√144=L (1)	√361=S (1)	
		√81=I (4)	√144=L (1)	√25=E (2)	√4=B (2)	
	√676=Z (4)		√1=A (1)	√4=B (2)	√361=S (3)	
	√225=O (4)		√441=U (2)	√4=B (1)	√16=D (3)	
	√196=N (4)	√324=R (2)		√196=N (3)	√1=A (3)	√4=B (3)
√1=A (4)						

			√324=R (1)			√484=V (3)
			√1=A (1)	√400=T (3)	√81=I (3)	
		√169=M (3)	√1=A (3)	√121=K (1)		
√36=F (2)		√81=I (3)	√361=S (1)	√25=E (1)	√25=E (2)	
	√225=O (2)		√196=N (3)	√121=K (2)		√49=G (4)
	√361=S (4)	√324=R (2)	√361=S (4)	√1=A (2)	√144=L (4)	
		√25=E (4)	√361=S (2)	√361=S (4)	√1=A (4)	

√324=R (1)						
	√25=E (1)	√625=Y (3)	√196=N (2)			√225=O (4)
	√400=T (1)	√324=R (3)	√81=I (2)		√529=W (2)	√324=R (4)
		√196=N (1)	√81=I (3)	√64=H (2)	√81=I (2)	√81=I (4)
		√81=I (1)	√1=A (3)	√256=P (1)	√400=T (2)	√49=G (4)
		√64=H (3)	√225=O (1)	√144=L (4)	√81=I (4)	
				√1=A (4)	√196=N (4)	

		√324=R (4)				
√9=C (1)		√625=Y (4)	√400=T (4)	√196=N (4)	√441=U (4)	
√361=S (3)	√81=I (1)		√81=I (2)		√225=O (4)	
√25=E (3)	√400=T (1)	√196=N (2)	√49=G (2)			√9=C (4)
√400=T (3)	√361=S (1)	√81=I (1)		√81=I (2)		
	√1=A (3)	√25=E (1)		√324=R (2)		
	√361=S (3)	√400=T (3)		√225=O (2)		

					√25=E (2)	
	√16=D (3)		√36=F (1)	√400=T (2)		√25=E (4)
	√400=T (1)	√1=A (3)	√81=I (2)	√1=A (1)		√484=V (4)
	√144=L (3)	√25=E (1)	√324=R (2)	√441=U (1)	√25=E (4)	
	√1=A (3)		√9=C (1)	√256=P (2)	√81=I (4)	
√361=S (3)				√144=L (4)	√361=S (2)	
			√4=B (4)	√25=E (4)		

			√49=G (4)	√25=E (4)	√25=E (4)	
			√324=R (4)	√25=E (2)		√196=N (4)
		√81=I (1)	√196=N (1)	√196=N (2)		√361=S (4)
		√9=C (1)	√81=I (2)	√64=H (1)	√25=E (3)	
	√225=O (2)	√400=T (2)		√400=T (1)	√196=N (3)	
√324=R (2)	√441=U (2)		√144=L (3)	√225=O (3)	√25=E (1)	
				√1=A (3)		

	$\sqrt{144}$=L (2)	$\sqrt{225}$=O (3)				
	$\sqrt{144}$=L (3)	$\sqrt{441}$=U (2)	$\sqrt{225}$=O (3)	$\sqrt{196}$=N (1)		
$\sqrt{36}$=F (3)		$\sqrt{36}$=F (2)	$\sqrt{324}$=R (3)	$\sqrt{16}$=D (1)	$\sqrt{25}$=E (1)	
	$\sqrt{49}$=G (1)	$\sqrt{16}$=D (2)	$\sqrt{225}$=O (1)	$\sqrt{361}$=S (3)	$\sqrt{361}$=S (1)	$\sqrt{25}$=E (4)
		$\sqrt{225}$=O (1)	$\sqrt{196}$=N (2)		$\sqrt{484}$=V (4)	$\sqrt{361}$=S (1)
			$\sqrt{81}$=I (2)	$\sqrt{225}$=O (4)		
				$\sqrt{169}$=M (2)	$\sqrt{400}$=T (4)	$\sqrt{361}$=S (4)

	$\sqrt{1}$=A (3)					$\sqrt{256}$=P (4)
		$\sqrt{169}$=M (3)				$\sqrt{324}$=R (4)
		$\sqrt{1}$=A (3)		$\sqrt{36}$=F (1)	$\sqrt{225}$=O (4)	
$\sqrt{81}$=I (3)	$\sqrt{676}$=Z (3)	$\sqrt{16}$=D (1)	$\sqrt{169}$=M (2)	$\sqrt{324}$=R (1)		$\sqrt{16}$=D (4)
$\sqrt{196}$=N (3)	$\sqrt{49}$=G (1)	$\sqrt{361}$=S (2)	$\sqrt{81}$=I (1)	$\sqrt{324}$=R (2)		$\sqrt{441}$=U (4)
	$\sqrt{49}$=G (3)	$\sqrt{25}$=E (1)		$\sqrt{225}$=O (2)	$\sqrt{9}$=C (4)	
				$\sqrt{16}$=D (2)	$\sqrt{25}$=E (4)	

				√324=R (4)		
					√25=E (4)	
	√196=N (3)				√196=N (4)	
√225=O (3)	√25=E (1)			√196=N (4)	√361=S (2)	
√81=I (3)	√196=N (1)	√81=I (1)		√400=T (2)	√1=A (4)	
√16=D (1)	√196=N (3)	√324=R (1)	√25=E (2)	√121=K (2)	√324=R (2)	√144=L (4)
	√361=S (1)	√441=U (3)	√36=F (1)		√81=I (2)	√256=P (4)

PAGE 72

√361=S (2)		√225=O (2)	√16=D (4)	√16=D (4)		
	√196=N (2)	√25=E (4)	√4=B (2)		√81=I (4)	
		√529=W (4)	√4=B (2)	√1=A (1)	√9=C (1)	√196=N (4)
	√25=E (3)	√81=I (2)	√144=L (1)	√121=K (1)		√49=G (4)
	√324=R (2)	√16=D (3)	√81=I (3)	√4=B (1)		
				√324=R (3)	√4=B (3)	

	√400=T (1)	√64=H (1)		√49=G (2)	√144=L (2)	√361=S (4)
√625=Y (1)	√49=G (1)		√196=N (2)		√1=A (4)	√25=E (2)
		√81=I (1)	√361=S (3)	√81=I (2)	√25=E (4)	
		√169=M (1)	√400=T (3)	√16=D (4)	√64=H (2)	
		√196=N (3)	√1=A (3)	√81=I (4)	√361=S (2)	
		√256=P (3)				

			√1=A (1)	√256=P (1)		
√324=R (2)	√361=S (2)		√324=R (1)		√361=S (1)	√144=L (3)
	√1=A (2)	√361=S (4)		√529=W (1)	√1=A (3)	
√25=E (2)		√25=E (4)		√169=M (3)	√81=I (3)	
√4=B (2)			√49=G (4)	√1=A (4)	√196=N (3)	
				√1=A (3)	√9=C (4)	

√121=K (3)	√9=C (3)					
		√81=I (3)		√36=F (1)	√144=L (1)	√196=N (4)
		√144=L (3)	√361=S (2)	√36=F (1)	√81=I (4)	√25=E (1)
	√9=C (3)		√256=P (2)	√1=A (1)	√1=A (4)	
			√529=W (1)	√225=O (2)	√324=R (4)	
		√144=L (2)	√225=O (2)			√400=T (4)

		√25=E (1)				
		√196=N (1)	√9=C (1)	√1=A (2)		
√324=R (3)	√400=T (1)	√484=V (3)	√324=R (2)	√324=R (1)	√144=L (2)	√324=R (4)
	√225=O (3)	√441=U (2)	√1=A (3)	√25=E (1)		√25=E (4)
		√400=T (2)	√256=P (1)	√144=L (3)	√49=G (4)	
		√1=A (2)	√81=I (4)	√196=N (4)	√36=F (3)	
		√36=F (4)	√196=N (2)			

				$\sqrt{144}=L$ (3)	$\sqrt{144}=L$ (3)		
		$\sqrt{324}=R$ (3)	$\sqrt{25}=E$ (3)	$\sqrt{81}=I$ (4)	$\sqrt{225}=O$ (3)		
			$\sqrt{256}=P$ (4)	$\sqrt{64}=H$ (3)	$\sqrt{196}=N$ (4)		
		$\sqrt{81}=I$ (1)	$\sqrt{169}=M$ (4)		$\sqrt{49}=G$ (4)		
	$\sqrt{400}=T$ (1)	$\sqrt{484}=V$ (1)		$\sqrt{441}=U$ (4)			
$\sqrt{9}=C$ (1)	$\sqrt{441}=U$ (2)	$\sqrt{225}=O$ (2)	$\sqrt{25}=E$ (1)	$\sqrt{100}=J$ (4)		$\sqrt{529}=W$ (2)	
$\sqrt{1}=A$ (1)	$\sqrt{400}=T$ (2)		$\sqrt{121}=K$ (2)	$\sqrt{324}=R$ (2)	$\sqrt{225}=O$ (2)		

		$\sqrt{144}=L$ (4)				
$\sqrt{25}=E$ (4)	$\sqrt{400}=T$ (4)	$\sqrt{225}=O$ (1)	$\sqrt{25}=E$ (4)	$\sqrt{529}=W$ (1)		$\sqrt{25}=E$ (3)
$\sqrt{25}=E$ (4)		$\sqrt{16}=D$ (1)	$\sqrt{225}=O$ (1)		$\sqrt{144}=L$ (3)	
	$\sqrt{4}=B$ (4)	$\sqrt{144}=L$ (2)	$\sqrt{361}=S$ (1)		$\sqrt{121}=K$ (3)	
	$\sqrt{144}=L$ (2)		$\sqrt{1}=A$ (2)	$\sqrt{196}=N$ (3)	$\sqrt{1}=A$ (3)	
	$\sqrt{25}=E$ (2)			$\sqrt{169}=M$ (2)	$\sqrt{441}=U$ (2)	
		$\sqrt{324}=R$ (2)	$\sqrt{4}=B$ (2)			

			√324=R (3)	√25=E (3)		√25=E (4)
	√9=C (4)	√1=A (4)		√400=T (3)	√144=L (4)	
		√625=Y (1)	√400=T (4)	√400=T (4)	√81=I (3)	
		√256=P (1)			√144=L (3)	
	√169=M (1)	√361=S (2)				
	√441=U (1)	√121=K (2)		√64=H (2)		
√4=B (1)			√25=E (2)	√25=E (2)	√9=C (2)	

		√361=S (4)				
	√25=E (4)	√144=L (2)	√25=E (1)	√144=L (1)		√16=D (3)
√196=N (2)	√25=E (2)	√400=T (4)	√400=T (1)		√196=N (3)	
√196=N (2)	√1=A (2)	√81=I (4)	√400=T (1)	√441=U (3)		
	√4=B (4)	√64=H (2)	√225=O (3)	√81=I (1)		
		√9=C (2)	√361=S (3)	√144=L (1)		

√361=S (3)			√64=H (2)	√196=N (2)	√196=N (4)	
	√144=L (3)	√196=N (1)	√25=E (2)	√9=C (2)	√225=O (4)	√361=S (4)
		√1=A (3)	√81=I (1)	√400=T (2)		√81=I (4)
		√36=F (1)	√324=R (3)		√81=I (2)	√400=T (4)
		√36=F (1)	√441=U (3)		√9=C (4)	√121=K (2)
		√144=L (3)	√441=U (1)	√169=M (1)		√1=A (4)
		√256=P (3)				

√361=S (4)						
	√196=N (4)		√169=M (1)	√529=W (2)	√324=R (3)	
		√324=R (4)	√225=O (2)	√1=A (1)		√25=E (3)
		√441=U (4)	√144=L (2)	√196=N (1)		√121=K (3)
	√4=B (4)		√361=S (1)	√144=L (2)	√9=C (3)	√196=N (1)
		√625=Y (2)	√25=E (2)	√81=I (1)	√225=O (1)	√81=I (3)
					√256=P (3)	

				√16=D (3)	√25=E (3)	
		√324=R (2)	√81=I (1)	√9=C (1)	√81=I (3)	
	√25=E (2)	√144=L (1)	√441=U (2)	√196=N (1)	√361=S (3)	
√324=R (4)	√49=G (4)	√9=C (2)		√400=T (3)	√25=E (1)	√256=P (1)
√196=N (4)	√25=E (4)	√25=E (2)		√441=U (3)		
√324=R (4)	√1=A (4)		√361=S (2)		√225=O (3)	

	√25=E (4)	√361=S (2)	√25=E (2)			
√324=R (4)		√64=H (4)	√361=S (2)		√196=N (3)	
	√400=T (4)	√1=A (2)	√361=S (1)	√225=O (3)		
	√49=G (2)	√1=A (4)	√81=I (3)	√121=K (1)		
		√25=E (4)	√400=T (3)	√324=R (1)	√400=T (3)	
	√529=W (4)		√1=A (1)	√1=A (3)		√361=S (3)
			√256=P (1)			

	√400=T (2)	√64=H (2)				
√169=M (2)			√144=L (1)			√1=A (1)
	√324=R (2)	√361=S (3)	√25=E (1)	√169=M (3)	√196=N (1)	
	√1=A (2)	√25=E (4)	√4=B (3)	√49=G (1)	√81=I (3)	√25=E (4)
	√576=X (4)	√529=W (2)	√324=R (4)	√9=C (4)	√144=L (3)	√361=S (4)
		√25=E (4)		√9=C (3)	√81=I (4)	

√4=B (2)	√441=U (2)	√25=E (3)		√144=L (4)	√25=E (4)	
√1=A (2)	√121=K (3)	√361=S (2)	√16=D (4)		√484=V (1)	
	√81=I (3)	√25=E (2)	√1=A (4)		√25=E (1)	
		√144=L (3)	√324=R (4)	√324=R (1)	√1=A (1)	√144=L (1)
	√1=A (3)			√9=C (4)	√4=B (1)	

√121=K (2)		√169=M (4)	√81=I (4)		√144=L (1)	
√361=S (2)	√196=N (2)	√361=S (3)		√400=T (4)		√1=A (1)
	√16=D (3)	√1=A (2)		√9=C (4)	√441=U (1)	√441=U (1)
	√196=N (3)	√4=B (2)		√169=M (1)	√81=I (4)	√400=T (1)
		√441=U (3)	√36=F (3)		√484=V (4)	

	√64=H (4)	√400=T (4)	√81=I (2)			√361=S (1)
		√121=K (2)	√441=U (4)	√196=N (2)	√196=N (1)	
	√64=H (3)	√9=C (2)	√225=O (4)	√81=I (1)	√49=G (2)	
	√1=A (2)	√400=T (3)	√1=A (1)	√361=S (4)		
√4=B (2)		√484=V (1)	√324=R (3)	√1=A (3)	√25=E (3)	

	$\sqrt{1}$=A (1)	$\sqrt{196}$=N (1)				
		$\sqrt{25}$=E (1)	$\sqrt{400}$=T (1)		$\sqrt{81}$=I (2)	$\sqrt{196}$=N (2)
	$\sqrt{225}$=O (3)	$\sqrt{169}$=M (1)		$\sqrt{49}$=G (2)		$\sqrt{81}$=I (2)
	$\sqrt{529}$=W (3)	$\sqrt{324}$=R (3)			$\sqrt{324}$=R (2)	$\sqrt{1}$=A (2)
$\sqrt{361}$=S (3)		$\sqrt{9}$=C (3)		$\sqrt{25}$=E (4)	$\sqrt{81}$=I (2)	
			$\sqrt{4}$=B (4)	$\sqrt{484}$=V (2)	$\sqrt{1}$=A (4)	$\sqrt{361}$=S (4)
						$\sqrt{121}$=K (4)

			$\sqrt{25}$=E (3)	$\sqrt{25}$=E (1)	$\sqrt{361}$=S (1)	$\sqrt{49}$=G (2)
		$\sqrt{196}$=N (1)	$\sqrt{144}$=L (3)	$\sqrt{484}$=V (1)	$\sqrt{196}$=N (2)	
			$\sqrt{25}$=E (1)	$\sqrt{121}$=K (3)	$\sqrt{81}$=I (2)	
$\sqrt{361}$=S (4)		$\sqrt{441}$=U (3)	$\sqrt{9}$=C (3)		$\sqrt{25}$=E (2)	
	$\sqrt{25}$=E (4)	$\sqrt{4}$=B (3)	$\sqrt{400}$=T (2)	$\sqrt{81}$=I (2)	$\sqrt{529}$=W (4)	
		$\sqrt{64}$=H (4)	$\sqrt{361}$=S (4)	$\sqrt{1}$=A (4)		

	√484=V (1)			√169=M (3)		
		√1=A (1)	√9=C (1)	√400=T (2)	√25=E (3)	
√361=S (4)	√49=G (4)		√64=H (2)	√441=U (1)		√144=L (3)
		√196=N (4)	√49=G (2)	√441=U (1)	√4=B (3)	
	√400=T (2)	√81=I (4)	√169=M (1)	√441=U (2)	√225=O (3)	
	√324=R (4)	√64=H (2)	√225=O (2)	√324=R (3)		
		√81=I (4)	√1=A (4)		√256=P (3)	

		√625=Y (4)		√1=A (4)		
			√196=N (4)	√121=K (2)	√256=P (4)	
		√400=T (1)	√9=C (2)	√169=M (4)	√1=A (2)	
		√1=A (2)	√225=O (1)	√225=O (4)	√49=G (2)	√625=Y (3)
	√256=P (2)	√441=U (1)		√9=C (4)	√676=Z (3)	√25=E (2)
	√9=C (1)				√1=A (3)	
√64=H (1)				√324=R (3)	√9=C (3)	

		√196=N (4)	√9=C (2)	√64=H (2)		
	√81=I (4)	√1=A (2)	√49=G (4)	√4=B (1)		
	√121=K (4)	√225=O (2)		√1=A (1)		
√1=A (4)	√324=R (2)				√196=N (1)	√400=T (3)
	√400=T (4)		√25=E (1)	√361=S (3)	√289=Q (1)	√196=N (3)
	√256=P (3)	√400=T (1)	√25=E (3)	√441=U (1)	√25=E (3)	
		√324=R (3)				

				√361=S (2)	√400=T (2)	
			√25=E (2)		√1=A (1)	
			√400=T (2)	√16=D (1)		√625=Y (1)
		√16=D (4)	√196=N (1)	√196=N (2)		
√144=L (3)	√81=I (4)	√25=E (4)	√225=O (2)	√441=U (1)		
√361=S (4)	√1=A (3)	√9=C (2)		√361=S (1)		
√324=R (4)	√25=E (4)	√49=G (3)	√25=E (3)	√144=L (3)		

√25=E (4)			√324=R (2)	√361=S (3)		
	√196=N (4)		√256=P (3)	√25=E (2)		
	√81=I (4)	√25=E (1)	√25=E (3)		√400=T (2)	
	√196=N (1)	√9=C (4)	√529=W (1)	√25=E (3)	√400=T (2)	
√25=E (1)		√81=I (4)	√144=L (3)			√25=E (2)
√324=R (1)		√361=S (3)	√16=D (4)			√4=B (2)
			√169=M (4)	√25=E (4)		

		√256=P (1)	√324=R (2)	√25=E (2)	√196=N (3)	
		√16=D (2)	√324=R (1)	√225=O (3)	√16=D (2)	√25=E (1)
	√196=N (2)		√25=E (1)	√81=I (3)	√324=R (1)	
	√441=U (2)		√400=T (3)	√256=P (1)	√1=A (1)	
√64=H (2)			√1=A (3)	√576=X (4)	√1=A (4)	√400=T (4)
		√361=S (4)	√25=E (4)	√196=N (3)		

	√1=A (2)		√256=P (4)			
√9=C (2)	√25=E (4)	√169=M (4)		√400=T (4)		
√9=C (2)	√400=T (4)	√144=L (1)	√1=A (1)	√49=G (3)	√1=A (3)	
√400=T (4)	√225=O (2)	√441=U (2)	√25=E (3)	√529=W (1)		√529=W (3)
	√1=A (4)	√361=S (3)	√196=N (2)	√625=Y (1)		
			√25=E (1)	√400=T (2)		
			√324=R (1)	√361=S (1)		

			√144=L (2)	√196=N (1)	√49=G (1)	
			√81=I (1)	√25=E (2)	√361=S (2)	
	√9=C (2)		√144=L (1)	√196=N (2)		
	√400=T (3)	√225=O (2)	√441=U (2)	√1=A (1)		
	√81=I (4)	√196=N (3)	√25=E (3)	√81=I (1)		
	√64=H (4)	√25=E (4)	√16=D (1)	√81=I (3)	√144=L (3)	√9=C (3)
√361=S (4)			√144=L (4)	√16=D (4)		

		$\sqrt{361}=S$ (1)			$\sqrt{36}=F$ (4)	
$\sqrt{196}=N$ (3)		$\sqrt{196}=N$ (2)	$\sqrt{25}=E$ (1)		$\sqrt{361}=S$ (1)	$\sqrt{25}=E$ (4)
	$\sqrt{49}=G$ (3)	$\sqrt{81}=I$ (2)	$\sqrt{484}=V$ (1)	$\sqrt{400}=T$ (2)	$\sqrt{225}=O$ (1)	$\sqrt{81}=I$ (4)
	$\sqrt{361}=S$ (3)	$\sqrt{81}=I$ (3)	$\sqrt{1}=A$ (2)	$\sqrt{144}=L$ (1)	$\sqrt{25}=E$ (2)	$\sqrt{144}=L$ (4)
	$\sqrt{361}=S$ (3)				$\sqrt{324}=R$ (2)	$\sqrt{25}=E$ (4)
		$\sqrt{1}=A$ (3)			$\sqrt{4}=B$ (4)	

						$\sqrt{81}=I$ (4)
		$\sqrt{324}=R$ (3)			$\sqrt{100}=J$ (4)	$\sqrt{196}=N$ (4)
$\sqrt{25}=E$ (1)	$\sqrt{625}=Y$ (1)	$\sqrt{361}=S$ (1)	$\sqrt{1}=A$ (3)	$\sqrt{1}=A$ (2)	$\sqrt{441}=U$ (4)	
	$\sqrt{324}=R$ (1)	$\sqrt{1}=A$ (1)	$\sqrt{25}=E$ (3)	$\sqrt{144}=L$ (2)	$\sqrt{441}=U$ (2)	$\sqrt{324}=R$ (4)
		$\sqrt{256}=P$ (1)	$\sqrt{81}=I$ (2)	$\sqrt{256}=P$ (3)	$\sqrt{289}=Q$ (2)	$\sqrt{25}=E$ (4)
			$\sqrt{256}=P$ (3)	$\sqrt{400}=T$ (2)		
			$\sqrt{1}=A$ (3)		$\sqrt{625}=Y$ (2)	

√25=E (4)	√9=C (4)					
	√196=N (4)	√25=E (2)	√196=N (2)		√196=N (1)	
	√256=P (2)	√1=A (4)	√361=S (2)		√225=O (1)	√361=S (3)
	√576=X (2)	√196=N (4)	√25=E (2)	√324=R (1)	√81=I (3)	√64=H (1)
	√81=I (4)	√25=E (2)		√361=S (3)	√400=T (1)	
		√36=F (4)		√1=A (3)		
				√225=O (3)		

	√1=A (1)					
		√256=P (1)		√625=Y (4)		
		√256=P (1)	√144=L (4)		√25=E (3)	
√625=Y (1)	√144=L (1)		√144=L (4)	√361=S (3)	√9=C (2)	
	√100=J (4)	√25=E (4)	√361=S (2)	√1=A (2)	√324=R (3)	
			√361=S (2)	√25=E (2)		√441=U (3)
						√256=P (3)

				√25=E (2)			
	√361=S (4)		√144=L (2)	√361=S (1)			
		√64=H (4)	√324=R (1)	√121=K (2)			
		√81=I (4)	√1=A (1)	√9=C (2)	√81=I (2)		
	√324=R (4)	√400=T (1)	√324=R (3)		√361=S (3)	√400=T (2)	
√400=T (4)		√361=S (1)	√1=A (3)	√16=D (3)			
			√9=C (3)				

						√1=A (1)	
		√169=M (1)			√529=W (1)		
√324=R (4)	√25=E (1)	√625=Y (2)	√225=O (1)	√196=N (2)	√25=E (1)		
√225=O (4)	√9=C (4)	√81=I (3)	√196=N (2)	√361=S (1)	√441=U (2)		
√400=T (4)	√1=A (3)	√225=O (4)	√400=T (3)		√36=F (2)		
	√529=W (3)	√16=D (4)	√81=I (3)	√196=N (3)	√49=G (3)		

√361=S (2)	√144=L (2)	√25=E (2)	√400=T (1)		√1=A (4)	
		√225=O (1)	√196=N (2)	√196=N (1)	√25=E (4)	√16=D (4)
		√441=U (1)	√196=N (2)	√25=E (1)	√324=R (4)	√169=M (4)
	√324=R (1)	√25=E (3)		√441=U (2)	√625=Y (3)	√81=I (4)
	√400=T (3)	√1=A (1)	√49=G (3)	√324=R (3)	√400=T (2)	
		√1=A (3)	√49=G (1)	√225=O (3)		
		√9=C (3)	√25=E (1)			

	√9=C (3)	√36=F (1)	√625=Y (4)			
√324=R (1)	√1=A (1)	√81=I (3)		√1=A (4)		√361=S (2)
√169=M (1)	√361=S (3)			√529=W (4)	√256=P (2)	
√361=S (3)	√81=I (1)			√225=O (2)	√4=B (4)	
√1=A (3)	√196=N (1)	√9=C (3)		√324=R (2)	√441=U (4)	
√49=G (1)	√144=L (3)			√361=S (4)	√9=C (2)	

					√324=R (4)	√25=E (4)
			√1=A (2)	√121=K (1)	√9=C (4)	
√49=G (3)	√25=E (2)	√16=D (2)	√225=O (1)	√144=L (2)	√81=I (1)	√196=N (4)
	√196=N (3)	√81=I (3)	√225=O (1)	√1=A (2)	√196=N (1)	√1=A (4)
	√529=W (3)	√64=H (1)	√9=C (2)	√49=G (1)	√16=D (4)	
	√361=S (3)		√361=S (2)			
			√25=E (2)			

						√144=L (1)
		√4=B (4)	√324=R (3)	√25=E (3)	√225=O (1)	√4=B (1)
		√441=U (4)	√144=L (4)	√49=G (3)	√529=W (1)	
	√324=R (4)	√324=R (2)	√441=U (2)	√25=E (1)	√196=N (3)	
√256=P (4)			√324=R (1)	√225=O (2)	√81=I (3)	
		√36=F (2)	√144=L (2)			√49=G (3)

$\sqrt{49}=G$ (1)						$\sqrt{16}=D$ (4)
$\sqrt{81}=I$ (1)			$\sqrt{25}=E$ (2)		$\sqrt{25}=E$ (4)	
	$\sqrt{36}=F$ (1)	$\sqrt{400}=T$ (1)	$\sqrt{144}=L$ (2)		$\sqrt{361}=S$ (4)	
		$\sqrt{49}=G$ (2)	$\sqrt{81}=I$ (1)		$\sqrt{25}=E$ (4)	
		$\sqrt{196}=N$ (1)	$\sqrt{49}=G$ (2)	$\sqrt{324}=R$ (4)	$\sqrt{484}=V$ (4)	$\sqrt{144}=L$ (3)
	$\sqrt{484}=V$ (3)	$\sqrt{49}=G$ (1)		$\sqrt{441}=U$ (2)	$\sqrt{25}=E$ (3)	$\sqrt{25}=E$ (4)
		$\sqrt{25}=E$ (3)	$\sqrt{361}=S$ (3)	$\sqrt{361}=S$ (3)	$\sqrt{100}=J$ (2)	

	$\sqrt{9}=C$ (2)					
		$\sqrt{64}=H$ (2)		$\sqrt{324}=R$ (4)		
		$\sqrt{25}=E$ (2)	$\sqrt{324}=R$ (3)	$\sqrt{25}=E$ (1)	$\sqrt{25}=E$ (4)	
$\sqrt{121}=K$ (2)	$\sqrt{9}=C$ (2)	$\sqrt{25}=E$ (3)		$\sqrt{324}=R$ (1)	$\sqrt{64}=H$ (4)	
		$\sqrt{400}=T$ (3)	$\sqrt{1}=A$ (1)			$\sqrt{400}=T$ (4)
		$\sqrt{361}=S$ (1)	$\sqrt{361}=S$ (3)	$\sqrt{4}=B$ (4)	$\sqrt{361}=S$ (3)	$\sqrt{225}=O$ (4)
			$\sqrt{25}=E$ (1)	$\sqrt{81}=I$ (3)	$\sqrt{324}=R$ (4)	

√361=S (1)			√144=L (2)	√25=E (2)		
	√324=R (1)	√144=L (4)	√4=B (2)	√9=C (4)	√324=R (3)	
	√4=B (4)	√225=O (1)	√81=I (4)	√4=B (2)	√25=E (3)	
	√441=U (4)	√196=N (1)		√4=B (3)	√81=I (2)	
	√256=P (4)	√64=H (1)	√225=O (1)	√4=B (3)	√324=R (2)	
			√225=O (3)			√16=D (2)
				√324=R (3)		

PAGE 112

		√64=H (4)				
	√49=G (4)	√100=J (1)	√225=O (1)	√361=S (3)		
√169=M (1)	√1=A (1)	√441=U (4)	√400=T (3)	√324=R (1)		
		√1=A (4)	√361=S (1)	√144=L (3)	√324=R (2)	
	√144=L (4)		√1=A (2)	√25=E (2)	√25=E (3)	√4=B (2)
				√361=S (2)	√400=T (2)	√4=B (3)

		√25=E (2)		√25=E (4)	√81=I (4)	
	√9=C (2)	√256=P (1)	√225=O (1)	√400=T (4)	√144=L (4)	√196=N (4)
	√361=S (1)	√1=A (2)	√144=L (2)	√225=O (1)	√144=L (4)	
		√49=G (3)	√121=K (2)	√256=P (1)		√441=U (4)
√400=T (3)	√64=H (3)	√196=N (3)	√81=I (3)	√9=C (2)		√4=B (4)
		√225=O (3)	√25=E (2)	√196=N (2)		
	√400=T (3)					

	√1=A (1)					
		√36=F (1)		√225=O (2)	√361=S (2)	
		√324=R (1)		√324=R (2)	√196=N (2)	
	√81=I (1)				√25=E (2)	
√1=A (1)	√9=C (1)	√256=P (3)		√400=T (2)		
	√64=H (3)		√144=L (3)	√25=E (4)	√169=M (4)	
	√1=A (3)	√1=A (4)	√49=G (4)	√1=A (3)		√225=O (4)

√400=T (4)	√25=E (4)		√9=C (4)			
	√196=N (4)	√81=I (4)	√1=A (4)	√529=W (2)		
		√324=R (3)	√4=B (4)	√81=I (2)		
			√81=I (3)		√484=V (2)	√324=R (3)
	√144=L (1)	√25=E (1)	√1=A (1)	√196=N (3)	√25=E (2)	√25=E (3)
			√484=V (1)	√324=R (1)	√49=G (3)	√361=S (2)
				√400=T (1)		

	√361=S (4)	√4=B (2)	√400=T (4)	√25=E (4)		
		√225=O (4)	√1=A (2)	√25=E (4)		
			√64=H (4)	√361=S (2)	√324=R (3)	
√144=L (2)		√9=C (4)	√16=D (1)	√25=E (2)	√36=F (1)	√225=O (3)
	√144=L (2)	√25=E (1)	√4=B (2)	√1=A (3)	√225=O (1)	√169=M (3)
		√1=A (2)	√144=L (1)	√441=U (1)	√324=R (3)